God in the Daily

GOD in THE DAILY

A 52-Week Guide to Seeing God Move in the Here and Now

RONDA PAULSON

GOD IN THE DAILY
A 52-Week Guide to Seeing God Move in the Here and Now

Copyright © 2026 by Ronda Paulson

Disclaimer: This book has been published for the purpose of providing the reader with general information on its subject matter. The author and the publisher believe the information to be accurate and authoritative at the time of publication. The book is sold with the understanding that neither the author nor the publisher is providing professional advice, and the reader should not rely upon this book as such. Every situation is different, and professional advice (whether psychological, legal, financial, tax, or otherwise) should only be obtained from a professional licensed in your jurisdiction who has knowledge of the specific facts and circumstances.

Scriptures taken from the Holy Bible, New International Version®, NIV®. Copyright © 1973, 1978, 1984, 2011 by Biblica, Inc.™ Used by permission of Zondervan. All rights reserved worldwide. www.zondervan.com. The "NIV" and "New International Version" are trademarks registered in the United States Patent and Trademark Office by Biblica, Inc.™

Cover Design by Carson Burchette
Interior Layout and Design by Brittany Becker
Editorial Team: Ezra Bayer, Traci Matt, Jamie Smith, Tessa Carvalho

ISBNs:
E-book: 979-8-89165-376-4
Paperback: 979-8-89165-377-1
Hardcover: 979-8-89165-378-8

Published by:
Streamline
Kansas City, MO
www.streamlinebookspublishing.com

To every Isaiah 117 House staff member, volunteer, LAT member, donor, local Isaiah 117 church supporter, local civic group supporter, lemonade stand holder, child welfare worker, and judge who believed in me before they should have, and in this mission before it had proven itself! And to all who have joined along the way. Thank you for listening to a God who still speaks, and moves, and heals, and redeems, and creates a way. May we always have eyes to see, ears to hear, a heart full of compassion, and feet ready to move into action.

Contents

Foreword

T HE FIELD OF neuroscience teaches us something both simple and profound: Our brains can change and adapt through repeated actions over time. This concept, known as *neuroplasticity*, reminds us that consistency has the power to transform us. Simple, intentional actions practiced over and over can rewire the very structure of our minds.

Think about the countless times you've driven home without remembering much of the drive itself. It's a little unsettling, yes, but also remarkable. It reveals that your brain has formed well-worn pathways through repetition—driving home has become second nature. It's a perfect picture of how repetition shapes who we are and how we live.

Any good trainer would echo this truth about our physical health as well. Transformation doesn't come from one trip to the gym or one healthy meal. It's born out of small, daily choices—those repeated actions over time that change not only our bodies but our habits, our mindset, and our way of living.

And perhaps this same principle holds true in our spiritual lives. Maybe transformation—the kind that draws us nearer to God and shapes us more into His likeness—happens not only in the big, extraordinary moments but also in the quiet, everyday seemingly small and simple ones.

I've often found myself waiting for God in the "big spaces": a moving worship service, a powerful conference, an inspiring event.

Those experiences can be beautiful and catalytic, no doubt. But I've come to wonder if the truest and deepest experience of life with God might actually unfold in the ordinary moments—the small, daily rhythms that make up most of our lives.

What if the way we are meant to know God most intimately is through those small, daily actions repeated over time? What if transformation happens as we learn to notice His presence not just in the mountaintop experiences but in the mundane—the commute, the dishes, the conversations, the quiet pauses in our day?

Because here's the truth this book reminds us of so beautifully: God is not distant. He is near. He is present in every ordinary moment. He's not waiting to meet us after we finish our to-do list or escape the noise of everyday life. He is already here, fully with us, fully aware, fully loving.

I'm confident this book will repeatedly and consistently remind you to look for him there. I trust you'll be delighted with what you find.

Jason Johnson
Director of Church Mobilization and Engagement
Christian Alliance for Orphans (CAFO)

Introduction

HEY FRIENDS!
I'm so glad you're here, and I want to welcome you to *God in the Daily*. Consider this the start of a journey we're about to take together. One where we find God's fingerprints in our everyday lives. If we were sitting across from each other right now, I'd hand you a cup of coffee and ask how you're doing. That is what I hope you feel in these pages. Two friends, thinking about ordinary life and how our God and His Word are faithful in all of it.

This personal journey of mine all began a few years ago. I had recently started a nonprofit, and a friend of mine was helping me with some marketing. She suggested that once a week I grab my phone and record a quick video to share what was going on with the ministry. I will be honest, I was not crazy about the idea. For one, I had never been on the Facebook!

But one Sunday, I decided I had to share all the ways I had seen God move that previous week. He was showing up day after day in such tangible ways, and I literally *had* to share! So I propped up my phone on a wobbling stack of books in my living room (the higher the camera, the skinnier you look) and recorded a quick, heartfelt encouragement to post online. Honestly, I was nervous and wasn't sure if anyone beyond my mom would even watch it! But I hit "upload," whispered a prayer, and hoped maybe one person would be encouraged.

Well, to my surprise, that little video wasn't watched only by my mom; friends started tuning in, and then friends of friends. Week by week, those simple *Sundays with Ronda* videos blossomed into something people looked forward to. I began hearing from all kinds of folks, each sharing that these Sunday moments lifted their spirits and often even called them to action!

Now, fast-forward to today, and that weekly rhythm has found its way onto these pages. That's how *God in the Daily* came to be. It's a devotional that carries the heart of those Sunday videos into a year-long journey. It follows a simple pattern of one story and reflection per week for a year. Each week, you'll find a personal story, Scripture, and some thoughts on how I spotted God in the midst of the everyday. You can read one entry each week and then meditate on that Scripture in the days that follow.

Life gets busy and messy. Believe me, I still have days when dinner is pizza and someone doesn't have clean underwear! But the beautiful thing is, God shows up in the middle of all that everyday chaos. So, friend, come as you are, and let's journey together. Bring your real self because that's exactly who God loves to meet.

As you read week by week, I hope you'll find yourself nodding along, maybe laughing, and seeing little glimpses of God's goodness in your own story. We'll walk through this year together, one week at a time, growing and learning as we go. We have divided the book into four parts: Winter, Spring, Summer, and Fall. So no matter when you pick up this devotional, you can turn to the current season and dive right in! No matter when you start, I am truly honored to be part of your weekly routine, cheering you on each step of the way. Are you ready? Let's go find God in the daily!

Winter

A God of Second Chances

Learn to do right; seek justice. Defend the oppressed.
Take up the cause of the fatherless;
plead the case of the widow.
—Isaiah 1:17

N 2014, MY husband, Corey, and I were training to become foster parents when we visited a child welfare office. I remember sitting in the conference room of that drab, cubicle-filled space and hearing that when children are removed from their homes, they often have to wait there for a foster placement.

I looked around at the sterile walls and fluorescent lights and imagined a frightened child sitting in that cold office, uncertain of their future. My heart broke at the thought. In fact, I learned that a little girl had actually slept in that very conference room the night before. I couldn't shake the image of how forgotten she must have felt. In that moment, I felt God whisper to my spirit, "These are My children. What are you going to do?"

It was a question I just could not shake. God was inviting me in. He wanted me to join Him in caring for His children on one of the worst days of their lives. Fast-forward one year to November 5, 2015. At 3:30 p.m., I received a call from a caseworker about a nine-month-old boy who needed a foster home immediately. Within an hour, Corey and I, along with our two kids, were picking up our foster son at the back door of a different but eerily similar child welfare office. He was dirty, dressed in clothes two sizes too small, and literally had a roach-infested diaper bag, with nothing else in the world.

As I cradled this scared little boy, my heart heard God's call a second time. I realized the question He asked me in that conference room was not going away. God was giving me another chance to answer His call to, as Isaiah 1:17 says, "Take up the cause of the fatherless." And although this little boy had a father, in that moment, in that office, he was fatherless.

That night, my mind swirled with what-if questions. I began to dream of a better way. A way to show these precious children God's love and hope right from the start. Some of the questions I asked were:

- What if there were a home where children could go immediately when they were removed from their families?
- What if it were a safe place with friendly, loving volunteers to care for them?
- What if there were clean clothes, bath toys, snacks, comfy beds, and teddy bears waiting for them?
- What if, instead of a cubicle, a traumatized child saw smiles, books, and snuggly blankets in a warm home?

I couldn't stop imagining it. I saw in my heart a welcoming home with a fully stocked kitchen, a cheerful girl's bedroom and a boy's bedroom, play areas, and bathrooms filled with supplies, all prepared in advance for "the least of these" (Matthew 25:40). I envisioned a team of volunteers on call to greet a frightened child with loving arms and reassure them that they are safe and not alone. Once I surrendered to God's call, things began to move.

We opened the very first Isaiah 117 House in 2018, turning that God-given vision into reality right in Carter County, Tennessee. From day one, our prayer was that every child who walked through our bright-red door would feel the opposite of forgotten. We wanted each little one to feel safe, worthy, and lavished with love from the moment they arrived.

God even wrote second chances into our personal story through this journey. The precious foster baby boy we picked up in 2015 became a permanent part of our family. In 2018, we adopted Isaiah and his younger brother, Eli, into our forever family. Every time I look at those boys, I'm overwhelmed at how God gave them and us a beautiful second chance at family. It reminds me that when we step out in obedience, God often blesses us in ways we couldn't imagine.

Today, I stand amazed at all God has done. What started as a single dream in one county has blossomed far beyond anything I imagined. There are now over forty Isaiah 117 Houses across thirteen states, each one providing a safe haven for children on their hardest day. And thousands of children have experienced love, comfort, and hope when they needed it most.

Through this journey, I have seen that God is a God of second chances. He didn't give up on calling me, even when I felt inadequate or unsure. And God is offering *you* a second chance as you start this fifty-two-week devotional. Maybe it's a restart in your faith journey or a second chance to step out and do something you feel He is nudging you to do. My story is proof that when we answer His call, even if it's on the second or third try, God can create something beautiful that changes lives.

Reflection Questions

- In what areas of your life do you sense God offering a "second chance" or a fresh start this year?
- Have you paused to ask God what He wants for you in this season? Take time to pray and listen for His direction.
- What practical step can you take today to align your plans with God's wisdom for your life?

Don't Miss God Because of a Screen

Teach us to number our days,
that we may gain a heart of wisdom.
—Psalm 90:12

SEVERAL YEARS AGO, I traveled with a group of energetic college girls and was floored by how much time they spent on their phones. We were in a van coming back from a dance competition, and instead of talking or soaking in the moment, they were just scrolling and scrolling and scrolling some more.

But just as soon as I started to feel the tiniest bit judgy, the Holy Spirit seemed to whisper in my ear, "Ronda, this is *you*. You're always busy, always moving, always texting." This broke my heart, and I knew there wasn't much I could say in response.

The truth was, I was always on my phone. Whether I was waiting at the doctor's office or standing in line at the store, I would instinctively distract myself instead of engaging with the people or world around me. And here I was, watching these young women do the same, missing what was right in front of them.

It made me think of that famous Super Bowl halftime meme of the kid looking at his phone when Justin Timberlake walked up behind him. People criticized him for being on his phone, but honestly, don't we all do that when we're uncomfortable? That kid was overwhelmed and did what children do. He reached for the security blanket of his phone. We adults are no better. We bury ourselves in screens to avoid awkward silence or difficult thoughts.

Sitting there in the van, God brought to mind Psalm 90:12, the cry of Moses: "Teach us to number our days, that we may gain a heart of wisdom." And the longer I meditated on this verse, the more convicted I became about all the precious time I wasted and the moments I missed because I'm consumed with trivial things.

This verse became my prayer for myself and those girls. Life is too short to be lived on autopilot or wasted on endless social media feeds. I want to wake up each morning and ask God to show me how to use my time for Him. Scrolling through someone else's vacation photos is harmless fun, sure, but God is calling me to more. He's calling me to *real* connections, *real* service, and *real* growth. And I don't want to miss it because I'm looking down at a screen.

When we ask God to help us number our days, we're really asking for perspective. To value each day and use it wisely. Wisdom might mean putting the phone down and being fully present with your family at dinner. It might mean saying yes to that prompting to visit a neighbor or no to an activity that isn't God's best for you.

Gaining a heart of wisdom starts with realizing time is a gift to steward, not an endless commodity. So this week, I challenge you to start treating your minutes and hours as valuable. Pray for the discipline to prioritize your tasks effectively so you don't regret how you spend your time this week and this year.

Reflection Questions

- What everyday distractions tend to consume your time? How might they be keeping you from something better God has for you?

- If you asked God to help you "number your days," what do you think He might prompt you to prioritize or change in your daily routine?
- What is one practical step you can take this week to be more present with God or with those around you (for example, setting aside your phone during certain hours)?

Sabbath Is a Gift

*Remember the Sabbath day by keeping it holy. Six
days you shall labor and do all your work, but the
seventh day is a sabbath to the LORD your God.*
—Exodus 20:8–10

NOT LONG AGO, I found myself at a breaking point, literally sobbing in a McDonald's parking lot while on the phone with my therapist. I had run myself ragged doing good things: pouring into our ministry, speaking, and parenting four kids. In my drive to serve, I had completely drained my own tank.

Finally, my counselor and our board lovingly cornered me. "Ronda," one of them said, "either you take a sabbath rest, or you're headed for a total crash." That's how spent I was. So, somewhat reluctantly, I obeyed the Lord's nudge and took a sabbatical. For nine weeks, I stepped back from ministry to renew my spirit and body. And you know what? God met me there in the rest and began restoring what burnout had broken.

During that season, I dove deep into studying sabbath and grew very convicted (there's that word again)! I realized that out of all Ten Commandments, the only one modern Christians seem to dismiss outright is "Remember the Sabbath day by keeping it holy."

We'd never say adultery or theft is okay, but resting for one day a week? That's optional. I had been guilty of that mindset myself. Hard work comes more naturally to me than stillness. Yet God commanded a sabbath for a reason. He knows our tendency to run ourselves into the ground. He literally built a rhythm of rest into creation because He loves us.

When I finally slowed down, I discovered how much I'd been missing. Things like unhurried dinners with my family, peaceful evenings without emails, quiet moments to actually listen for God's voice. It was like rain on dry ground.

Today, I am a passionate sabbath advocate. As a family, we've started guarding Friday sundown to Saturday sundown as our sacred time. We light candles, read Scripture about rest, and take communion together. We unplug from screens and schedules and simply be.

Believe me when I say this is not an easy routine. The world will throw every obstacle to keep you from resting. But we persevere because we've tasted the sweetness of it. I'm learning that sabbath is not a luxury or legalism; it's a gift. God's inviting us to live in His rhythm of grace instead of the world's relentless grind.

Exodus 20:8 says, "Remember the Sabbath day by keeping it holy." The word "remember" tells me this isn't something to forget or ignore. God literally commands us to stop our labor and trust Him. If the Creator of the universe could rest on the seventh day, who am I to think I don't need it? In practicing sabbath, I'm finding freedom. Freedom from the lie that everything depends on me working, freedom to enjoy God and my loved ones with my whole heart. It's an act of trust to lay down my to-do list for twenty-four hours, but each time I do, I'm declaring, "God, You are in control, not me." There is holy beauty in that stillness.

So this week, I encourage you to remember the Sabbath day and receive God's gift of rest. Let it refresh your soul for this coming week.

Reflection Questions

- Do you regularly take time to rest and recharge, or do you feel guilty when you're not productive? Why do you think that is?

- What would it look like for you to "remember the Sabbath" in your life? Consider a practical plan for a day of rest this week.
- How might trusting God with your unfinished work for one day actually deepen your faith and bless your family?

From Milk to Solid Food

*Anyone who lives on milk, being still an infant, is not
acquainted with the teaching about righteousness. But
solid food is for the mature, who by constant use have
trained themselves to distinguish good from evil.*
—Hebrews 5:13–14

ONE DAY, I was preparing a talk and revisited a familiar
Scripture about spiritual growth. You know, the one about
how when we're new believers, we start with spiritual milk,
but as we mature, we move on to solid food. I've heard that verse a
million times, but suddenly I saw it through a fresh lens.

I began reflecting on the process of weaning a child. As a mom of
four, believe me, I've lived that drama. The baby crying in the night
for a bottle, and me gently refusing because it's time for them to learn
to sleep without milk. In that moment, the baby is furious!

"Why, Mom? You've always given me what I wanted before. Where's
my milk?!" From the infant's perspective, I'm withholding comfort
for no reason. But I know the reason. I know that moving past the
bottle is ultimately best for my child.

Can I admit something? In my walk with God, I've often been
like that weaning baby. Early in my faith, I'd pray, and God would
answer in obvious, immediate ways. My "milk." I came to expect that
comfort every time I cried out. But as I grew, there were seasons God

didn't answer the way I wanted or when I wanted.

Doors closed that I desperately wanted open. At times, I found myself crying, "Father, where's the answer I'm looking for? Why aren't You coming through this time?" It felt, honestly, like God might be withholding something good from me. But could it be that He was allowing a season of weaning, not to be cruel, but to help me grow up? A loving parent sometimes withholds what a child wants in the moment to give them what they truly need long-term.

That realization was like a light bulb coming on. The pattern was there in Scripture all along. Think of Abraham and Sarah, waiting decades for a promised child. Or the Israelites, longing for deliverance. Even in my own life there were times I prayed for something and got silence, only to later see God was growing my character or redirecting me to something better.

Spiritual maturity means trusting God's wisdom even when I don't get the "milk" right away. It's moving from a Santa Claus view of God (Give me what I ask for, pronto!) to a deeper understanding that sometimes no or not yet is an expression of His love. Just as I wasn't abandoning my baby by ending midnight bottles, God isn't abandoning me when He says wait. He's helping me learn to rely on Him in a new, richer way, feeding me solid food for my soul.

Hebrews 5:13–14 says, "Anyone who lives on milk, being still an infant, is not acquainted with the teaching about righteousness. But solid food is for the mature." This Scripture challenges me to embrace growth. Milk is comforting and easy; solid food can be harder to chew. Likewise, some truths in God's Word or experiences in life are challenging to digest. But if we want to mature spiritually, we must allow God to grow us beyond a surface-level faith.

This week, remember that the Father hasn't forgotten you. He's feeding you differently to strengthen you. Solid food may not be as sweet as milk at first taste, but it will nourish you for the long haul.

Reflection Questions

- Can you recall a time when God didn't answer a prayer the way you hoped? Looking back, what might He have been teaching or developing in you during that "weaning" season?
- In what areas of your faith do you feel God is calling you to "grow up" or trust Him more deeply?
- How can you remind yourself this week that God's delays or denials may actually be His loving preparation for something greater?

When Stress Strikes

Cast all your anxiety on him because he cares for you.
—1 PETER 5:7

A FEW YEARS AGO, I broke out in a horrible stress rash. I'm talking head-to-toe hives that itched like crazy. Cute, right? Nothing screams "I need a break" like your skin staging a revolt! The timing was ironic because outwardly, everything in our ministry was going great. We were opening new Isaiah 117 Houses in multiple states, donations were coming in, and miracles were happening. Yet on the inside, I was wound up tight, internalizing every new challenge. My body finally said, "Enough." There I was in Georgia for a big benefit concert, covered in hives and finally admitting to myself and God: *I'm not handling this well.*

That week, in the throes of discomfort, God gently revealed something: I had been praying about my stresses, yes, but I hadn't truly been releasing them to Him. I'd unload my worries in prayer, then pick them right back up and carry them around all day. No wonder I was a mess!

In my hotel room, slathered in anti-itch cream, I felt God inviting me to a new posture. Literally, a posture on my knees each morning. I decided that every day, first thing, I would kneel, thank God for who He is, and then physically lay down my burdens before him. It sounds simple, but that intentional act has been transforming me.

There's something about actually kneeling, an outward sign of inward surrender, that helps my heart let go.

I realized, too, that God wasn't *forcing* me to come to Him with my worries; He was *inviting* me. Like a patient father, He was waiting for me to say, "Lord, I can't carry this. Please help." All the while I was frantically scratching and maybe complaining a bit, He was ready with open arms. Sometimes it takes a breaking point (or a rash!) to get us on our knees. But oh, the peace that flooded in once I truly submitted!

My circumstances didn't instantly change. There were still deadlines, budget needs, and children to care for. But I changed. By starting the day in humility and prayer, I found a new strength to face whatever came. I'm learning to live out 1 Peter 5:7, casting all my anxiety on him, because He cares for me.

This verse shows us that God isn't annoyed by our worries. He wants us to bring them to Him, like a dad bending down to take a heavy backpack off his tired child's shoulders. When we hold on to anxiety, we're like that child insisting on lugging an unbearable load alone. Our Father says, "Please, let Me carry that. I care about every fear and frustration you have." I had to reach the end of my rope to truly believe this.

Now, each time I feel the itch of stress rising, literally or figuratively, I try to pause and pray, "Lord, I give this to You again." It's not one and done; surrender is a daily practice. But God's care is constant. So if you are weighed down this week, know that Jesus is gently calling, "Let Me take that burden." He loves you so much and never intended you to fight anxiety alone.

Reflection Questions

- What worries or stresses have been keeping you up at night or giving you metaphorical "hives"? Take a moment to identify them honestly.
- How do you typically handle stress? Do you pray about it, distract yourself, or try to control everything? What might it look like to truly cast those anxieties onto Jesus?

- Consider a tangible action, like kneeling in prayer or writing your worries on paper and laying them before God, to symbolize giving your burdens to Him. How could this physical act help deepen your trust that God cares for you?

When Challenges Become Blessings

*Whoever wants to be my disciple must deny themselves
and take up their cross daily and follow me.*
—LUKE 9:23

AS A FOSTER mom and now adoptive mom, one question I hear a lot is, "But what about your biological kids? How has fostering affected them?" I understand the concern, because parents naturally worry how our choices will impact our children. I've had those fears myself.

My son Mac was an only son until we started fostering, and I knew it stretched him. In fact, when he recently wrote his college application essay about his biggest challenge, he chose to write about our family doing foster care. He was candid about the hard parts: being jealous when a new little boy arrived and soaked up everyone's attention, feeling sad watching grandparents dote on that child, and fearing his place in our family might be lost.

Reading those lines, my heart clenched. No mother likes to see her child struggle. Part of me thought, *Oh Lord, what have we done to him?*

But then Mac's essay took a turn. He wrote, "Honestly, it wasn't long before that foster brother just felt like my brother." The real challenge, he said, came when he realized he could love this little boy wholeheartedly and still have to say goodbye if the child returned home. Loving with risk of loss—now that's a challenge for anyone, let alone a teenager. I kept reading, tears in my eyes, as my son described how that situation changed him.

"My biggest challenge has become my biggest blessing," he wrote. "It has forever changed me as a person and the way I view the world. It's made me kinder. It's made me not judge. It's made me realize you don't know what's going on in someone's home or life. It's made me welcoming to others and taught me that acts of kindness matter." At this point, I was openly sobbing over my laptop!

Mac concluded, "I see now that we are called to step in and help. When you do that, it changes you." Wow. I couldn't have said it better. Here I was worrying about protecting my kids from hardship, but God was busy shaping their hearts through it. The very things that challenged my son—sharing his home, risking heartbreak—became the catalyst for his growth in compassion, empathy, and faith.

It hit me that this is exactly how God works. Jesus told us plainly that following Him involves taking up our cross daily. That sounds like a test, and it is. But on the other side of that cross is resurrection. The more we give ourselves away in love, the more we experience God's blessings. Maybe not in comfort or ease, but in meaning, joy, and intimacy with Him. Our family's "hard" became our "holy."

By opening our home to foster children, Mac did lose some comforts and took on fears of loss. Yet he found a bigger life. One filled with brotherly love, purpose, and an awareness of God's heart for "the least of these." This week, if you're facing a challenge in doing what's right, such as forgiving someone, serving in a new way, or standing up for justice, remember that God can turn that challenge into your greatest blessing. Carrying a cross is never easy, but it draws us closer to the One who carried the cross for us.

Reflection Questions

- Can you think of a time when a difficult or uncomfortable step of obedience to God resulted in unexpected blessings or personal growth for you?
- What "cross" might Jesus be asking you to take up daily right now? It could be a responsibility, a calling, or an attitude to surrender. How might embracing that challenge draw you closer to Him?
- How does knowing that others before you have faced challenges by faith encourage you to persevere in your own difficult situations?

Sunday 7:

The Lord Will Fight for You

The LORD will fight for you; you need only to be still.
—Exodus 14:14

OFTEN JOKE THAT I'm a Sullivan East High School graduate, which around my area means I might have a little "redneck" fight in me. I grew up scrappy, quick to argue, and determined to win any showdown. In fact, I'm excellent at fighting. Not the hand-to-hand kind, but the hold-my-earrings, let-me-tell-you-why-you're-wrong kind.

For years, I saw this as a strength. After all, sometimes you need to stand up and battle, right? But lately Jesus has been tapping me on the shoulder, reminding me that His way is so very different. He's been whispering to my heart, "Ronda, it's not about winning arguments. It's about winning with love."

Let me give you an example. Not too long ago, I found myself getting all riled up over a situation at the local Walmart. If you've ever people-watched at Walmart, you know it can test your sanctification! Someone was rude, and I could feel my inner "redneck" itching for a showdown.

But then I heard that gentle nudge from Jesus, urging me to hold my tongue and choose grace. It's funny, I can quote the stories of Jesus cleansing the temple and think, "See, He flipped tables! He got fiery!" But when I actually study Scripture, I notice Jesus showed righteous anger toward hypocrisy inside the religious circle, but He consistently showed compassion and gentleness toward those outside. The aggressive driver who cuts me off, the grumpy cashier, the person on Facebook with the infuriating political post—those are precisely the people Jesus calls me to respond to with kindness, dignity, and respect.

It's not that there's never a time to confront wrong or stand for truth. But I'm learning that how I fight matters. Exodus 14:14 has become a theme verse in this season. It says, "The LORD will fight for you; you need only to be still." Ouch. Be still? But I have such a good comeback! Yet God says, "Let Me handle it."

When I insist on having the last word or proving I'm right, I might win the argument but lose an opportunity to show Jesus's love. Instead, if I stay still, zip my lips, and let God work, He can defend me far better than I could defend myself. And often, He diffuses situations in ways my sharp retorts never could.

I've watched Him turn an enemy into a friend, a misunderstanding into a ministry, all because I stepped back instead of swinging. It's humbling but also freeing. The pressure's off me to fix everyone. My job is simply to love others, and trust God to do the heavy lifting of changing hearts.

This verse from Exodus is a powerful reminder that often the most faith-filled action is inaction. It's refraining from reacting in our flesh. Being "still" doesn't mean we become doormats; it means we actively trust God's justice and mercy to prevail in His timing.

Reflection Questions

- Think of a recent conflict or irritation you faced. How did you respond? In hindsight, what might it have looked like to "be still" and let the Lord fight for you in that situation?
- Why is it so hard to hold back and stay gentle when we feel provoked or wronged? What would trusting God to defend you look like in a very practical sense (for example, not replying to an angry comment, or choosing to forgive rather than retaliate)?

- Who is one "difficult person" in your life you can commit to responding to with Christlike love and patience this week? Pray for God's help to repress any unholy anger and reflect Jesus to them.

Sunday 8:

Love, You're Not Alone

*The virgin will conceive and give birth to a son, and they
will call him Immanuel (which means "God with us").*
—MATTHEW 1:23

AT ISAIAH 117 House, we have a slogan painted on the
wall that says, "Love, you're not alone." It's simple, but it
resonates with every person who walks through our red
door. I think it resonates because deep down, none of us wants to
be alone in our pain.

We all crave someone to step into our story and say, "I'm here. I
care." I remember standing on the porch of one of our Houses as a
teenager arrived. He'd been through unspeakable trauma, and as our
team welcomed him with warm smiles and open arms, this tough
young man just crumpled into sobs, repeating, "Thank you, thank
you . . . " He realized in that moment he wasn't alone. There were
people who loved him, strangers even, because God loved him first.
It was holy ground.

That phrase "you're not alone" isn't just a nice sentiment; it's the
heartbeat of the gospel. The entire narrative of Scripture shows God
making sure we're not alone. In the Garden of Eden, God walked
with Adam and Eve in the cool of the day. Humanity's first experience
was God's companionship. When sin broke that intimacy, God still
did not abandon His people. He manifested His presence as a pillar

of cloud by day and fire by night with the Israelites. He fed them manna from heaven.

Then came the ultimate answer: Jesus, whose very name Emmanuel means "God with us." Jesus walked our roads, felt our sorrows, and touched our wounds. He assured His followers, "I am with you always, to the very end of the age" (Matthew 28:20b). And when He ascended, He sent the Holy Spirit to live in us, and birthed the church, a community commissioned to carry His love to every lonely corner of the world. Talk about a comprehensive plan to ensure we're not alone!

Knowing this, I feel such urgency that no one within my reach should suffer alone. It's why our Houses exist, so a scared child doesn't wait in a sterile office but rather in a cozy home with loving volunteers. It's why I try to look neighbors in the eye and ask how they're doing, why our family seeks out those who might not have anyone else.

If "Love, you're not alone" is God's message, I want it to be my life's message too. And let's be real, I have days I feel alone or unseen in my struggles. In those moments, I cling to the truth that God is right there with me, and I push myself to reach out instead of withdrawing. Often, He sends comfort through a friend's text or a song that comes on the radio at just the right time, reminding me of His promises. He's creative like that.

From the moment of Jesus's birth, God broadcast loud and clear: "I am with you." This week, if you are feeling lonely or overwhelmed, remember that Jesus has not left you. You are not alone. His Spirit and His people are a prayer away. Don't be afraid to raise your hand and say, "I need someone," because that's exactly what the body of Christ is for. Love will meet you where you are.

Reflection Questions

- Can you recall a time when someone made you feel deeply seen and supported in a hard time? How did their presence or kindness reflect God's love to you?

- Who in your life or community might be feeling alone right now? What is one concrete way you could reach out so they know someone cares?
- When you feel lonely or isolated, what promises or reminders help you re-center on the truth that God is Immanuel and always with you?

It's Always Been Our Calling

*Religion that God our Father accepts as pure and faultless
is this: to look after orphans and widows in their distress
and to keep oneself from being polluted by the world.*
—James 1:27

ONE EVENING AFTER sharing at a church about Isaiah 117 House, a woman came up and said, "What your ministry is doing by taking in these vulnerable children is just so Christian." She meant it kindly, but it got me thinking. Caring for orphaned and abandoned children isn't a *new* Christian idea; it's who we've been since the beginning!

In the earliest days of the church, the Roman world had a horrific practice. Babies who were unwanted, often due to deformity or mere preference for a different gender, were left in designated spots to die or be taken by slave traders. And what did the Christians do? They made those grim places their mission field. Historical accounts tell of believers who would go to those dumping grounds, rescue the infants, and raise them as their own sons and daughters. They couldn't stand by while little lives were discarded.

When I first learned that piece of history, it resonated deeply. Here we are two-thousand years later, and the ways children are abandoned have changed. In most places, it is more bureaucratic now, but the calling of God's people to care for the vulnerable hasn't changed one bit. "It's always been our calling," I found myself saying out loud one day.

Christians have historically stepped up to love the fatherless, welcome the stranger, and care for those society casts off. We were the ones founding orphanages, hospitals, and schools. Not because we're extra nice, but because Jesus compels us to. James 1:27 lights the way and says, "Religion that God our Father accepts as pure and faultless is this: to look after orphans and widows in their distress and to keep oneself from being polluted by the world." We aren't reflecting God's heart if we ignore the vulnerable. It's as simple and challenging as that.

I feel this calling in my bones. When I see a child lugging a trash bag of belongings into a social services office, I don't think, "Oh, poor them." I think, "That's my calling to make sure that child knows they are loved and not alone." And I'm overjoyed to see the church rising up again in our day.

A while back, multiple people came to me after a service, sharing their own stories: a man remembering his cousins spending twelve hours in a child welfare office, a woman who adopted a teen who arrived with nothing but the clothes on her back. These folks weren't jaded or bitter about the brokenness they'd seen; they were mobilized. I drove home that day with tears in my eyes, thanking God for letting me witness His people answering the ancient call anew.

We don't care for the vulnerable to earn brownie points with God. We do it because it is who we are! The early Christians understood this, and it set them apart in a cruel world. In our modern context, living out this calling this week might mean becoming a foster parent or supporting those who are, mentoring a teen in care, donating, advocating for systemic change, or simply showing up for someone in crisis. There are many ways to heed the call. What matters is that we do it, with each of us asking, "What's my part to play in this holy tradition of love?" Because caring for those in need isn't just a niche ministry for a few. It's the family business of all God's children, and it always has been.

Reflection Questions

- When you hear the biblical call to care for orphans, widows, and the oppressed, what stirs in your heart? Is there a specific group of people or an individual God is highlighting for you to "take up the cause" for?
- Consider the heritage of faith: Christians of the past who rescued abandoned infants or fought injustices. How do their stories inspire you to live out your faith more boldly?
- What is one action step you can take to "defend the oppressed" or support a child in need? It could be volunteering, giving, mentoring, or simply educating yourself and others. Remember, no step is too small when offered to God.

Sunday 10:

Do More than Pray

*Do not merely listen to the word, and so
deceive yourselves. Do what it says.*
—JAMES 1:22

SEVERAL YEARS AGO, when the COVID-19 pandemic hit
and lockdowns began, I started seeing a particular plea all over
social media: "Pray for the children who aren't safe at home."
With schools closed, many at-risk kids were suddenly trapped in
abusive or neglectful situations, invisible to teachers or coaches who
might normally help.

My heart broke reading those posts. Even our governor highlighted
the issue, forming a task force to find these hidden, hurting children.
Yes, pray, I thought, *but we can't stop at praying.* Because prayer, while
powerful, was never meant to be an excuse for passivity. Our hands
and feet must follow our knees.

One *Sundays with Ronda* video I actually recorded midweek because I couldn't hold it in. I looked into the camera and begged fellow
Christians to do something. I told them that if they knew a child
in their neighborhood or congregation who might be unsafe, they
should check on them.

I gave examples: Honk from the driveway and have the parent step
out to chat from a distance, drop off a meal or groceries if needed,
and keep your eyes and heart open. Yes, social distancing made it

tricky, but love finds a way within the rules. We simply could not sit in our comfortable homes and hope "those" kids would be alright. James 2:17 echoed in my ears: "Faith by itself, if it is not accompanied by action, is dead." If we claim to follow Jesus but do nothing when children suffer, what does that say about our faith?

I know fear and uncertainty can paralyze us, even when we're not going through a pandemic. "What if I intrude? What if I'm wrong?" But I'd rather risk awkwardness than live with regret that I stayed silent. The truth is, we all can do something. In that video, I said, "This is not the government's responsibility. This is our responsibility."

James 1:22 reminds us to not merely listen to God's Word, but to do what it says. Being a doer might mean making a phone call to report suspected abuse or rallying resources for a struggling single mom so she doesn't reach a breaking point. It means our faith gets its hands dirty. And let me tell you, I saw people respond.

During the pandemic, Isaiah 117 House supporters mobilized with porch drop-offs of supplies, extra check-ins with foster families, and creative safe activities for kids. Prayer was the fuel, but then we put feet to those prayers. And God moved through that combination of prayer plus action.

1 John 3:18 says, "Dear children, let us not love with words or speech but with actions and in truth." It's important to pray. Many battles are won first in the prayer closet. But biblical love always eventually leaks out into action. The Apostle John basically says in that verse, "Talk is cheap; real love shows up." In the parable of the Good Samaritan, two religious folks likely prayed for the injured man as they passed by, but only one man stopped to help—and Jesus said, "Go and do likewise" (Luke 10:37b).

This week, "doing likewise" may look like inconvenient, sacrificial involvement in someone's messy situation. It can be as straightforward as providing a meal, or as involved as becoming a mentor or foster parent. Not everyone's called to do the same thing, but we're all called to do something. So, yes, let's pray fervently. But then, as we say "Amen," let's listen for God's reply, because often, He's sending us to be the answer to the very prayer we just prayed.

Reflection Questions

- Have you ever felt the urge to help in a situation but hesitated because you weren't sure what to do or feared overstepping? What happened, and what can you learn from it?
- James 1:22 reminds us to be doers of the Word, not hearers only. What is one issue or need in your community or church that you frequently pray about? How might God be nudging you to become part of the answer to that prayer?
- "Do More Than Pray" isn't suggesting prayer is unimportant. Rather, it's highlighting that true prayer should spur us to act when we can. How can you integrate prayer and action in your life more intentionally?

Stepping Out in Faith

All these people were still living by faith when they died.
They did not receive the things promised; they only saw
them and welcomed them from a distance, admitting
that they were foreigners and strangers on earth.
—HEBREWS 11:13

RECENTLY, IN CHURCH, we studied Hebrews 11, the famous "faith chapter," which highlights heroes like Noah, Abraham, and Rahab. I've read it countless times, always focusing on the "By faith, [insert Bible hero] did [insert amazing feat]" parts. But this time, my eyes landed on the in-between verses, specifically Hebrews 11:13–16.

It hit me that all these great men and women of God stepped out in faith *without* seeing the end results. They obeyed God's call not knowing how the story would wrap up. Abraham never saw the multitudes that would descend from him. Moses never entered the Promised Land. They moved forward with only God's promise in hand, trusting that even if the fulfillment lay beyond their lifetime, it was worth it. They understood they were "foreigners and strangers on earth," living for a heavenly country.

This realization spoke directly to my heart. You see, when I obeyed God's call to start Isaiah 117 House, I had no clue what I was doing or how it would turn out. There was no blueprint for a ministry that provides an alternative for kids on removal day. It was just a dream and a ton of unanswered questions. People asked, "How will you fund it? What about liability? Will agencies even let you help?" and my honest answer was, "I'm not sure, but I feel God asking us to try."

We took it one step at a time, one house at a time, much like those Hebrews 11 heroes who took one step into the Red Sea or one step onto the unknown path. There were days I thought, "Lord, this makes no sense. It's too big, too hard." And in truth, I haven't seen the end of the story yet. Seven years in, we have over sixty locations in thirteen states (mind-blowing!), but I know God's still writing the story far beyond what I'll witness. And that's okay. My job isn't to see the finale; it's to be faithful in my chapter.

Walking by faith can be exhausting. I joke that this calling makes me feel closer to Jesus than ever and also makes me want to pray for Him to come back tomorrow, because it's so hard sometimes! There are days I'm weary of the brokenness: children hurt by those who should love them, bureaucratic hurdles, endless needs.

In those moments, Hebrews 11 encourages me. It reminds me that not seeing immediate results doesn't mean my faith is futile. Those saints "did not receive the things promised; they only saw them and welcomed them from a distance." Yet God was proud to be called their God. Why? Because they trusted Him enough to obey without guarantees.

I want to live that kind of faith. The kind where God could say, "I'm not ashamed to be her God, because she's not living for this temporary world anyway." If all I ever see are seeds planted and never the full harvest, it will be enough to know I did what my loving Father asked of me. Stepping out in faith is ultimately about trusting God's character.

The story God is writing through your faithfulness this week is part of a much bigger story that spans generations. Your obedient "yes" today might be the foundation for miracles years from now. So take heart and keep walking, even into the unknown. God walks with you each step, and He will make it count for eternity.

Reflection Questions

- Has God ever prompted you to do something that didn't fully make sense or was focused on an outcome you couldn't see? How did you respond, and what did you learn from that experience?
- What fears or uncertainties tend to hold you back from stepping out in faith? Write them down and then write a truth from God's Word next to each one.
- Consider a step of obedience you feel God might be asking of you right now. What would it look like to say "yes" even if you don't see the whole path?

One Person at a Time

*A new command I give you: Love one another. As I have
loved you, so you must love one another. By this everyone
will know that you are my disciples, if you love one another.*
—JOHN 13:34–35

WHILE I'M CONSTANTLY amazed at what God is doing through Isaiah 117 Houses, sometimes I catch myself thinking, "Lord, if this is Your work, why isn't it happening faster? These kids needed help yesterday." But as I look around this beautifully decorated home, ready to welcome children who need it, I realize something: God's plan is unfolding exactly as planned, with one person at a time saying "yes" to His call.

I think of our Knoxville, Tennessee, location, where two women, unbeknownst to each other, both felt the tug in 2019 to change how foster care begins in their community. Each could have dismissed it as an impossible dream, but instead, they each took one step by visiting our original Carter County home. There, God connected them (surprise!) and they teamed up.

Then a local coffee shop owner said "yes" to hosting an interest meeting. A newly relocated lady named Kristy heard about it and came, looking for friends but finding a mission. A judge lent his influence. Volunteers showed up to clean and paint. Donors gave what they could. Piece by piece, over four years, what started as two separate whispers in two women's hearts became a tangible house of hope.

Standing in it now, I see not just drywall and furniture, but the fingerprints of dozens of everyday heroes. It reminds me of our Savior. He came as one baby, grew up, and changed the world one interaction at a time—healing one leper, touching one outcast, calling one tax collector. Three years of those one-on-one moments, and the world was never the same.

The world today is noisy and chaotic. It's easy to feel like we're drowning in bad news and enormous problems. I get overwhelmed, too, with stories of abuse, systemic issues, violence, and so much suffering. But God gently refocuses me: "Just love the person in front of you, Ronda." One person at a time.

It might be a teen mom who needs a cheerleader. A caseworker who could use a coffee and a "thank you." A lonely neighbor. I can't fix everything, but I can love someone in Jesus's name today. And who knows what chain reaction that might spark? Jesus changed the world one life at a time, and He invites us to do the same.

The grand mission of God is accomplished in a million small, faithful actions by His people. Jesus illustrated this when He said giving a cup of water to one of "the least of these" is as if we did it for him. So when you feel insignificant or like your contributions don't matter this week, remember that every time you love one person well, you are part of God's big story. The world is indeed changed one person, one "yes," at a time. Keep saying yes. Keep loving the next one. In God's hands, your "little" becomes part of something so much bigger than you can imagine.

Reflection Questions

- Can you think of an instance when someone's small act of kindness or "yes" to God had a big impact on your life or on others? How does that encourage you regarding your own small acts?

- Who is one person in your life or vicinity that God may be asking you to focus on loving and serving right now? What's one practical way you can show them Christ's love this week?
- When you feel overwhelmed by the world's needs, what helps you refocus on the actionable mission right in front of you? How can remembering Jesus's example of engaging one by one shape your approach to ministry or daily life?

Pass the Wine Parenting

In the same way, after the supper he took the
cup, saying, "This cup is the new covenant in
my blood, which is poured out for you."
—Luke 22:20

LET ME SET the scene. It's the Last Supper, Jesus's final meal with His disciples. The mood is heavy; He knows what's coming. He also knows one of His closest friends at the table will betray Him within hours. What does Jesus do?

In that culture, there was a marriage proposal tradition where a man would pour a cup of wine and offer it to the woman. If she drank, she accepted the covenant. At this supper, Jesus takes a cup of wine and offers it as the new covenant in His blood, essentially extending an offer of unbreakable love to His "bride," the disciples. And yes, Judas is still sitting there. Jesus offers love even to the one who would hurt Him. He had washed Judas's feet earlier that evening, and now He includes him in the covenant gesture. Talk about radical love.

Several years ago, I was having a hard parenting week. The kind that leaves you crying in the bathroom, texting a friend, "Please pray before I lose it." One of our teenagers was pushing every boundary, rejecting our affection, and generally being porcupine-level prickly.

I felt my heart retreating behind walls of frustration and hurt. It's exhausting to keep pouring out love when it's not returned or even wanted. In the midst of this, our pastor shared the Last Supper insight that Jesus essentially "proposed" love to His followers with that cup, knowing full well one would betray Him and others would scatter. He still chose to love lavishly. That hit me hard. If my Lord could "pass the wine" to a man like Judas, I can certainly pass grace to my struggling teen.

So I tried something. Instead of lecturing or responding with the same coldness I was receiving, I gently told my child, "Nothing you do will make me love you less. I am here for you, even if you're angry." I offered a literal cup of hot cocoa as a peace offering (not wine, don't worry!), and we sat in silence for a bit.

Slowly, the walls came down. Not completely, but the atmosphere shifted. I saw, in those guarded eyes, a flicker of relief, maybe even hope. They expected me to retaliate or withdraw; instead I was saying, I'm not going anywhere. This is the heart of God for us. We can kick and scream, we can reject Him, yet He still stands at the door and knocks, offering fellowship.

Being still might mean biting your tongue during a teenager's tirade and whispering a prayer instead of snapping back. It might mean consistently showing up with love even when it's not acknowledged. God fights for our kids and loved ones in unseen ways; our role is to remain faithful in love. Jesus demonstrated that commitment to us both at the Last Supper and on the cross—loving forgiveness offered even as nails were driven in.

This week, when it's hard to love, remember how Jesus loved you at your worst, and let this realization refuel your commitment to love others through their worst. So here's to "passing the wine" of covenant love in our homes and relationships—an unconditional commitment that says, "I'm for you, and I'm not giving up." In doing so, we mirror the One who never gives up on us.

Reflection Questions

- Think of a time you've felt rejected or hurt by someone you were trying to love. How did you respond, and what do you learn from Jesus's example at the Last Supper about how you could respond in the future?

- What are some practical ways you can communicate unconditional love to someone who is difficult to love right now?
- How does remembering God's undeserved love for you in your lowest moments help you extend grace to others in theirs?

Spring

Hope in the Darkness

Why do you look for the living among the dead?
He is not here; he has risen!
—Luke 24:5b-6a

'LL NEVER FORGET one special Easter morning with my family on the Florida coast. We had decided to wake up before dawn and watch the sunrise over the ocean on Resurrection Sunday. Bleary-eyed and clad in hoodies, we trudged through the sand in darkness. As the sky began to blush pink, the kids fidgeted and yawned.

To be honest, I wondered if dragging everyone out of bed was worth it. But then, it happened. The sun peeked over the horizon in a burst of gold. Light danced on the water, and the whole world seemed to exhale.

In that moment, with the waves whispering and the sky ablaze, I felt something profound and realized this is what Mary Magdalene must have felt on the first Easter. I imagined her despair on the way to the tomb, and then her heart-pounding joy when she heard the angel announce, "He is not here; he has risen!" Everyone else had given up hope, but Mary showed up, and the Son rose before her eyes.

It's one thing to celebrate Easter in theory; it's another to feel hope breaking into darkness in your own soul. As I watched the darkness turn to day, I thought about how Easter is God's ultimate second chance for all of us. Jesus's resurrection means our worst day is never the last word. Death doesn't win. Sin doesn't win. Even despair doesn't win.

Because Jesus lives, new beginnings are possible. As I sat in my beach chair, tears welled up, and I silently thanked God for the second chances He's given me. Second chances at motherhood through adoption, at purpose after seasons of doubt, and at life itself through Jesus. "Easter is a promise of a new beginning," I found myself whispering.

Back at our condo later, while the kids devoured chocolate bunnies, I opened my Bible to John 21. That's where the resurrected Jesus gently restores Peter, the disciple who had denied Him three times. Jesus cooks Peter breakfast on the beach (gotta love our Savior's style) and gives him a threefold chance to affirm his love.

It struck me that Easter isn't just one day; it's a whole new reality. It means Jesus comes to the very people who failed Him and says, "Do you love Me? I still have work for you. Try again." If Peter could go from shame to leading the early church, what might God do with us, flaws and all? Easter tells me nothing—not my mistakes, not my losses, not even death—is beyond the redeeming power of Jesus. There's always hope of a new morning.

This week, whether you're basking in sunshine or walking through shadows, remember that the resurrection light dawns in the darkest places. It burst forth in a graveyard, after all! Jesus specializes in turning our graves into gardens, our mourning into dancing. So lift your eyes. The Son has risen, and because of Him, today is never too late for a fresh start.

Reflection Questions

- Think of an area in your life that feels like a "tomb." Maybe a situation that seems hopeless or dead. How does the truth of Jesus's resurrection speak to that situation?
- In what ways have you experienced second chances or new beginnings in your life? How can remembering those renew your hope for the future?

- How can you carry the hope of Easter into your everyday routines and challenges, not just on Easter Sunday but throughout the year?

57

God Wants to Use Us

And we know that in all things God works
for the good of those who love him, who have
been called according to his purpose.
—ROMANS 8:28

A FEW YEARS AGO, my weekly schedule looked like a logistical jigsaw puzzle. A golf fundraiser Friday, speaking at a little country church Sunday morning, another church Sunday night, then zipping between county meetings midweek. By Wednesday, I felt equal parts exhausted and exhilarated. In the thick of it, something amazing happened at a church in Greeneville, Tennessee.

After my talk, the pastor pulled me aside and shared an insight from Romans 8:28. We all know the verse as, "God works for the good of those who love him. . . ." But this pastor had heard a Bible teacher suggest a small translation tweak, one that blew my mind. The idea is that God works all things for the good of His people through His people. In other words, we are often the instruments God uses to bring about the good He's promised.

I sat with that thought for a moment. *Through his people?* Wouldn't it be just like God to invite us into His miracles! The NIV translation we're familiar with says, "in all things God works for the good of those who love him, who have been called according to his purpose." But imagine adding "through His people." It emphasizes God's plan to include us in His work. I felt a little like a schoolgirl hearing she's been picked for the team.

It reminded me of elementary school days playing Red Rover. (Confession: I was always picked first for Red Rover; as it turns out, a girl built like a linebacker with a competitive streak is very handy for breaking through handholds!) Being chosen felt great back then. But how much more humbling and amazing is it that the God of the universe chooses *us* to be on His team, warts and all?

If you're like me, you might sometimes think, "Sure, God works things for good, but He'll use someone holier, or more qualified. Not *me*." I see my flaws daily. I can be impatient, I overcommit, I sometimes forget important details (like that one time when I may have shown up at a meeting in two different shoes). It's easy to conclude that my weaknesses sideline me from God's A-team. But then I remember how God has always operated. He picked a stuttering Moses to confront Pharaoh, a shepherd boy David to be king, a band of fishermen to carry the gospel. He delights in using imperfect people because it showcases His power and grace.

Every success story of Isaiah 117 House has happened through ordinary folks saying "yes" to God's nudge. Volunteers, donors, foster families, and church partners. None of us alone could orchestrate such good. But together, guided by God, we become channels of His blessing.

The same God who doesn't need our help still chooses to involve us, like a father letting his young child "help" bake cookies. The batter might get messy, but the joy and bonding are priceless. God could do all His work solo and far more neatly, but instead He says, "Come on, be part of this!" He knows we'll learn and grow through the process, and the victory will be that much sweeter because we experienced it with Him.

So this week, if you ever doubt your significance in God's plan, let Romans 8:28 reassure you. Yes, he's working all things for good, and yes, He wants *you* in on the action. Your talents, your story, even your struggles can become the very tools through which God brings hope to others.

Reflection Questions

- What abilities or life experiences do you have that you've discounted, thinking "God can't use that"? How might those very things be channels for God's work to bless someone?
- Can you recall a situation where God brought about something good in someone's life through your small act of obedience or kindness? How does that encourage you to step out again?
- When you feel "not good enough" to serve God's purpose, what promise or truth from Scripture can you hold on to as a reminder that God gladly works through ordinary people?

Sometimes There Are No Words

Rejoice with those who rejoice;
mourn with those who mourn.
—ROMANS 12:15

HAVE YOU EVER felt like you have no words for the situation you're going through? I learned this in a big way years ago on September 11, 2001. At the time I was a young high school teacher. That morning, the principal's voice crackled over the intercom, urging us to turn on the TV. My students and I watched in stunned horror as the second plane hit the Twin Towers.

Those kids looked to me for answers an adult should have, and I had none. We all sat in that classroom together, speechless. There was nothing to say in that moment. All we could do was be there for each other, and it struck me deeply that presence mattered more than any explanation.

Fast-forward to my work with Isaiah 117 House, and the same truth echoes. We often receive children on what might be the worst day of their lives. In those moments, no pep talk or "right words" can fix things. What does help is sitting beside them, offering a hug or a hand to hold, and just staying with them in the hurt. We've had kids who arrive so angry or distraught that they can barely speak. For someone like me, who tends to fill silence with chatter, it's a discipline to hush up and simply listen, or even just share the silence. But it's a holy discipline, because it reflects what Jesus Himself did.

Consider Jesus at the tomb of His friend Lazarus. Before He did any miracle, He first wept alongside the mourners. No preaching, no immediate solution. Just tears and empathy. Or think of Job's friends who sat with him on the ground for seven days in silence because his grief was so great (Job 2:13). They got it right until they opened their mouths and started offering bad advice! Their silent presence was the true comfort. These examples remind me that when people are suffering, they don't need my advice or spiritual platitudes nearly as much as they need my compassionate presence.

Recently, a dear friend lost her husband, and as I walked into the funeral home, I felt that familiar anxiety: *What do I say?* I rehearsed a few sympathetic phrases in my mind, but when I hugged her, all I managed was, "I'm so sorry. I'm here with you." And maybe that was enough. I ended up just sitting next to her, occasionally handing her tissues, mostly just listening. There were stretches of quiet where neither of us spoke. And in the quiet, God's love was there, tangible in a gentle pat on the back or a shared tear.

One of the most powerful ministries you can offer is the ministry of presence. A cup of coffee together in silence, a ride home from the hospital, or simply a nod and eye contact that says, "I see you, and I'm not going anywhere." Those moments speak a thousand words without a single syllable. There's a time to encourage with words, yes. But often the initial healing comes when someone feels heard and held, not lectured or fixed. So this week, choose to enter into someone else's joys and sorrows, simply sharing the moment, which sometimes means saying nothing.

Reflection Questions

- Can you recall a time when someone's presence helped you more than any words could have? How does that shape the way you approach friends or family in pain?
- When faced with a loved one's tragedy or struggle, do you feel pressured to come up with answers? How might you

instead practice the ministry of presence and "mourn with those who mourn"?

- Think of someone in your life who is hurting right now. What's one way you can be there for them this week to assure them they're not alone?

They Carried the Mat

Two are better than one. . . . If either of them
falls down, one can help the other up.
—ECCLESIASTES 4:9–10

SEVERAL YEARS AGO, I did something radical for this tired mom of four. I went on a girls' getaway with my college roommates. No kids, just us middle-aged "girls" laughing, crying, and reminiscing in a cozy barn-turned-cabin in Kentucky. Let me tell you: Two days of heart-to-heart talks and belly laughs with women who have known me since I rocked scrunchies and oversized rugbys did wonders for my soul! It also brought to mind one of my favorite Bible stories about friendship.

In the Gospel of Mark, there's a paralyzed man who desperately needs healing. He has four fantastic friends who refuse to let crowds or obstacles stop them. When they can't get through the packed doorway to see Jesus, these guys literally climb the roof, cut a hole, and lower their friend down right in front of Jesus. Talk about determination and creativity! Jesus, seeing their faith, heals the man both spiritually and physically. I've always loved that story, but after this weekend with my lifelong friends, it hit even closer to home.

We all need friends like that man had. Friends who love us as we are, yet care too much to leave us stuck in our pain. My college gals and I have been carrying each other's "mats" for decades. We've seen each other through bad breakups, the loss of parents, scary health issues, job crises, and plenty of parenting drama. There were times one of us couldn't muster a prayer on her own because she was just that overwhelmed. That's when the others stepped in to pray for her, to encourage her, or sometimes just to say, "You rest—we've got you." Much like those four friends hauling their buddy up the roof, my friends have hoisted me up in my weak moments and carried me to Jesus when I didn't have the strength.

Mark 2:3–5 describes it beautifully when it says, "Some men came, bringing to him a paralyzed man, carried by four of them. . . . When Jesus saw their faith, he said to the paralyzed man, 'Son, your sins are forgiven.'" Notice it was the friends' faith and action that made the difference! This shows me that our faith isn't just a private thing. Sometimes we believe on behalf of each other when someone is too weary to believe on their own.

Not only did those friends love the paralyzed man, but they were also determined to help. They encountered a literal roadblock and thought outside the box—or rather, above the box! I chuckle imagining if it were a group of women. Would we have busted through a roof? (We might've at least tried the windows first!) But determination looks like whatever it takes to get your friend to the feet of Jesus. It might not be as dramatic as climbing a roof; it could be persistently praying for a friend every day for a year. It could be gently dragging a depressed friend out of the house for a change of scenery or sending encouraging Scriptures via text to a friend struggling with doubt.

As I reflected on my friendships, I also asked myself: Am I being that kind of friend to others? It's easy to enjoy the fun parts of friendship, but true Christian friendship sometimes calls for heavy lifting. Sometimes it means inconvenient love, like midnight phone calls or intervening when you see a friend heading down a harmful path. Only Jesus can heal and restore. Your job this week is to simply help others get to Him.

Reflection Questions

- Do you have friends in your life who "carry" you spiritually or emotionally when you're struggling? Take a moment to thank God for them and maybe send them a note of gratitude.
- Can you think of someone who might need you to be a determined friend right now, helping them draw closer to Jesus or find healing? What's one practical way you could do that?
- Reflect on a time you felt carried by someone else's faith or prayers. How can that experience inspire you to do the same for others who are paralyzed by fear, doubt, or hurt?

We Are Called to Go Out

Therefore go and make disciples of all nations. . . . And surely I am with you always, to the very end of the age.
—MATTHEW 28:19–20

LOVE VISITING NEW locations. Several years ago, I was at a kickoff luncheon for a new Isaiah 117 House, and I was buzzing with excitement. Not just because of the incredible $93,600 raised in an hour (though I did pinch myself over that!) but because of what I saw God doing.

A local committee member remarked to me, "I've never seen anything like this. People just grab hold of this mission and run with it!" As she spoke, I realized why this Isaiah 117 House movement resonates so deeply: It taps into the very core of our Christian calling. The emphasis is not on me or a well-executed strategy but rather the fact that caring for children in need is an essential part of who we're meant to be as Christ's followers.

Somewhere along the way, many churches became very inward focused. Lots of potlucks, programs, and events to keep the members happy on the inside, while occasionally saying, "Y'all invite a friend if you want." But Jesus didn't tell the *world* to come to church; He told the *church* to go to the world.

That Indiana luncheon reconfirmed for me that when believers hear about a mission like loving foster children and supporting broken families, something in our spiritual DNA leaps up and says, "Yes, this is right!" Why? Because it's straight from Scripture. James 1:27 says, "Religion that God our Father accepts as pure and faultless is this: to look after orphans and widows in their distress. . . ." We've been called to go out and be the hands and feet of Jesus to the vulnerable.

Standing at that luncheon, I shared how in Isaiah 1:17 God says to "take up the cause of the fatherless." We aren't doing something new; we're joining an ancient, God-ordained mission. And boy, did that room of folks respond! Grandmas, businessmen, and college students across generations and backgrounds were on fire to do their part. I saw tears in the eyes of a tough-looking contractor as I described a child sitting in a government office with a trash bag of belongings. Compassion is contagious when it aligns with God's heart.

It made me reflect on the early church in Acts. They didn't wait for people to walk into a synagogue and ask about Jesus. They went out preaching in marketplaces, homes, and streets. They shared food, met needs, and then shared Jesus. We can do the same in our time. Maybe it's not on a dusty road in Jerusalem, but it could be in a social worker's office, a foster care info meeting, or a community center. We go to where the hurt is, rather than expecting the hurting to find us.

If you're reading this, maybe your "go out" this week isn't about foster care per se. Perhaps God is nudging you to go out to the homeless in your city, or to mentor youth, or to simply step outside your close-knit friend circle and welcome a newcomer. Going out doesn't always mean traveling far or making grand gestures. It can mean stretching the borders of your comfort zone right where you are. The point is a posture of willingness to leave the familiar for the sake of the gospel. Jesus sends us out, but never alone.

Reflection Questions

- In what ways have you felt the church (or your own life) become too inward focused? How might Jesus be calling you to step outside the walls and go out to share His love?

- What is one need in your community (orphans, the elderly, the hungry, etc.) that stirs your heart? How could you get involved or support that cause as a way of living out James 1:27?
- "Going out" can be intimidating. What encouragement do you find in Jesus's promise to be with us as we go (Matthew 28:20)? How does the Holy Spirit empower you personally to serve others?

Control Your Anger with Love

*A new command I give you: Love one another. As
I have loved you. . . . By this everyone will know
that you are my disciples, if you love one another.*
—JOHN 13:34–35

SOMETIMES I HAVE more anger in me than I'd like to admit. A while back, there was a week where life handed me four separate opportunities to lose my cool, and I took the bait each time. First, there was a frustrating situation at a juvenile court where I literally envisioned myself flying through the air to throat-punch a particular person (not my finest fantasy).

Then, a blowup with one of my teenagers at home, where I channeled some "righteous anger" à la Jesus in the temple. Next, a spat with my dear hubby (I hate to say it, but I was wrong and had to choke down my pride on that one.). Finally, a road rage flare-up thanks to a lady who gave me the stink eye when I exited through an entrance due to a gas station traffic jam. By the end of the week, I had to laugh or else I'd cry at how quickly I could become combat-ready.

So I took these incidents to God and asked, "What is going on with me?" And He reminded me of a simple but crucial truth: Love is the only way to change hearts. Shaking my head in scorn at someone or barking at them about how wrong they are will not draw them closer to Jesus. It might, in fact, push them further away. We have to go out into the world *differently* than the world comes at us. Where the world is harsh and condemning, we're called to be gentle and compassionate.

I pictured that woman at the gas station. She didn't know me or understand how my frantic day had caused me to enter the wrong way. All she saw was a van doing something incorrectly, and she responded with scorn. And her response immediately made me defensive and angry. Similarly, the person in juvenile court probably had zero clue why I care so fiercely about these foster kids, and my intense approach likely irritated her. In neither case would me delivering a lecture or a snarky comment accomplish anything for Jesus. As much as my flesh wanted to "set people straight," I heard the Lord whisper, "That's *My* job. Your job is to love."

Jesus modeled this so well. Yes, He flipped tables that one time, but that was to call out wrong motivations of religious hypocrites who should've known better. With the regular broken, lost people, Jesus was remarkably patient and kind. He spent time with prostitutes and tax collectors, not to berate them but to show them a better way. He defended the woman caught in adultery from her accusers and gently told her, privately, to sin no more. He spoke with respect and tenderness to the woman at the well, even though she'd had five husbands. If anyone had a right to do the whole headshake "tsk-tsk" thing, it was Jesus. But with those outside the faith, He chose compassion over condemnation every time.

I realized that in my four anger scenarios, the two where I have solid loving relationships (with my daughter and husband) resolved with growth and sweetness. On the flip side, the two situations with people who don't know me would only be worsened by me unloading my anger. Without a relationship of love or understanding, confrontation just breeds more conflict. That old saying "people don't care how much you know until they know how much you care" is popular because it's true. If we want to make an impact for Christ "out in the world," it starts with people feeling seen and loved, not judged.

So this week, if you're tempted to get angry, pause and say, "Lord, how can I respond with love or wisdom here?" The world's got enough people shouting and shaking fists; it needs more people shining with grace.

Reflection Questions

- Think of a recent situation where you were angered or offended. In hindsight, how might a gentle or loving response have been more effective in showing Jesus's character?
- Are there specific triggers that tend to bring out a harsh reaction in you? What is one strategy to "pause and pray" before responding next time?
- How can you balance standing for what is right with doing so in a spirit of love?

Sunday 20:

Faith over Fear

When I am afraid, I put my trust in you.
—Psalm 56:3

WHEN I AM afraid, I put my trust in You." That singsong Scripture has echoed in our home for years. It's actually my daughter Sophie's life verse, taught to her as a little girl to calm her fears. We even turned it into a goofy family jingle complete with my son's off-key "oh, oh" at the end.

Yet for all our singing, I sometimes find myself acting out of fear even as an adult. Just recently, I caught myself doomscrolling news and feeling my stomach knot up. My thoughts raced with what-ifs about my kids, our ministry, and the world. Fear can pounce out of nowhere. I might be in the middle of a quiet evening or a casual social media check, and suddenly, I'm envisioning worst-case scenarios. Can you relate?

One week, my pastor preached on not living in fear. His sermon reminded me that God did not give us a spirit of fear (2 Timothy 1:7) and that as Jesus-followers, we can operate from a place of peace knowing Christ has overcome. Sitting there, I felt a gentle conviction (and yes, Sophie's little verse was looping in my mind). If I truly trust God, why do I let fear run wild in my head? The truth is that fear is a liar. It tells me I'm on my own when I'm not. It tells me disaster is certain when God is still sovereign and good.

After church, I decided to practice what I preach to my kids. Each time a fearful thought popped up that week, I intentionally paused and prayed: "Lord, I feel afraid of ____, but I choose to trust You with it."

Instead of suppressing the fear or spiraling with it, I'm learning to acknowledge it and then hand it to Jesus. Sometimes I literally open my hands and say, "Here, Lord, this worry is Yours." Do I instantly feel brave and peaceful? Not always. But I do feel less alone. I remember that the God who calmed storms and defeated death is with me in every fearful situation.

One of my favorite scenes in Scripture is when the disciples, terrified, think they are seeing a ghost as they see Jesus walking on water. He speaks peace over them: "Take courage! It is I. Don't be afraid" (Matthew 14:27). Those words weren't just for wind and waves two thousand years ago; they're for us today. Jesus is still saying, "It's Me here. You don't have to fear." When I am afraid, I have a choice: Listen to the fear or listen to my Father. Fear shouts worst-case scenarios. The Father whispers, "I am with you always." I want to choose His voice every time.

So here's my challenge for you this week. The next time fear knocks, answer with faith. Quote a promise from God's Word out loud. Hum a little Psalm 56:3 tune if you must. Remind your soul that God has brought you through every bad day so far, and He's not about to quit now.

Reflection Questions

- Name one recurring fear or anxiety you struggle with. What practical step could you take to "answer with faith" when that fear arises?
- Can you recall a time in the past when you sensed God's presence or help in a scary situation? How does remembering that experience encourage you to trust Him now?
- Read 2 Timothy 1:7. In what areas of your life do you need God's power, love, or self-discipline to replace a spirit of fear? Pray and invite Him into those areas this week.

A God Who Saves and Doesn't Shame

Therefore, there is now no condemnation
for those who are in Christ Jesus.
—ROMANS 8:1

'LL NEVER FORGET the day I received a message from a case-worker that left me in tears. They said, "We've already found a placement for this teen, but he really needs to experience an Isaiah 117 House." That single sentence was a culmination of so much prayer, dreaming, and hard work. It was as if God whispered, "See? This is what it's all about."

We arranged for that teenage boy to spend a few hours at our Isaiah 117 House despite having a foster home lined up, just so he could get a taste of the love and peace we offer. And he broke down. This tough, street-hardened kid sobbed tears of release and muttered thank-yous as our volunteers lavished him with kindness, hot food, and a safe space to rest. In a short time, he experienced what it means to not be judged or condemned but, rather, simply loved.

Driving home later, I reflected on how every person, whether a foster child or not, really needs an "Isaiah House experience." By that I mean, a moment where they encounter grace with no condemnation attached. You see, lately the kids coming to us aren't the cherubic toddlers and cute babies. We are seeing more teens with really heavy trauma.

They've been abused, they've fallen into addiction, and they carry guilt and shame. The world often looks at them and just sees trouble. But when that caseworker said this teen "needed to experience" our house, I knew what she meant. He needed a place where he wouldn't get a lecture or side-eye, but a hug and a sandwich. A place where, even if only for a night, he could breathe without fear of rejection.

I think of Jesus and the people He encountered. He was basically a walking Isaiah House. The woman caught in adultery is a prime example. Dragged before him by men ready to stone her, she undoubtedly expected condemnation. Yet after dispersing her accusers, Jesus said, "Neither do I condemn you. . . . Go now and leave your life of sin" (John 8:11). No condemnation, just grace and an invitation to a better life.

If Jesus chose mercy over condemnation, how much more should I, a recipient of His mercy, do the same? If He doesn't condemn me, why on earth would I think it's my job to condemn anyone else? My job is to love and show grace. Period. God can handle any necessary heart conviction or change in His timing. He's far better at it than we are.

The early church had a saying, "Come as you are." I fear sometimes today's church has projected, "Clean up your act, then you can belong." So this week, let's flip that script back to the way Jesus intended. And as we help others experience even a drop of unconditional love, I pray they'll be drawn to the Source of it in me: Jesus, who never shames us but saves us.

Reflection Questions

- Do you recall a time someone showed you grace when you expected judgment? How did that impact you?
- Who in your life might be craving an "experience" of love without strings attached? What's one way you could extend that to them?

- Pray for wisdom to show Christlike compassion and Christlike holiness in a way that people feel loved, not condemned.

Sunday 22:

Cancel the Chaos

*"Martha, Martha," the Lord answered, "you are
worried and upset about many things, but few things
are needed—or indeed only one. Mary has chosen what
is better, and it will not be taken away from her."*
— LUKE 10:41–42

AS SOMEONE WHO is always running and doing, it's hard for me to admit when I'm running too hard. A while back, after committing to post one *Sundays with Ronda* video a week, I woke up one Monday morning with a text that said, "Where was my *Sundays with Ronda* video?"

This made me do a double take because I'd forgotten it was even Sunday! At the time, I was juggling my nonprofit work, a college teaching job, and family life with four kids. The days bled together in a blur of to-do lists.

When I realized my lapse, I had a mini panic attack. If you know me, you know I'm the woman who tries to keep all the plates spinning. Admitting I dropped one felt like failure. That week, however, became a turning point. I nearly lost it trying to do everything. It was as if God allowed me to hit a wall to get my attention. And boy, did He ever get it. I sensed Him saying in no uncertain terms, "You cannot continue living at this pace, Ronda. Something has to give."

85

I wrestled with that because I loved all the things I was doing. Stepping away from any of it felt like quitting or letting God down. Oh, the irony. As if God needed me to run myself ragged for His sake. Eventually, through prayer and counsel, I made a hard decision: I resigned from my beloved teaching job. I intentionally canceled a major commitment from my calendar.

Talk about scary! I had been so accustomed to running on adrenaline and coffee that I wasn't sure who I was without the constant hustle. But within days of stepping off that hamster wheel, I physically and mentally exhaled in a way I hadn't in years. I was still busy with ministry and kids, of course, but there was breathing room again. I hadn't realized how close I'd been to burning out completely. In my attempt to "do it all," I was actually shortchanging everything. My family got a frayed, frazzled mom. My team got a stretched-too-thin leader. And God? Well, He got a Martha scurrying in the kitchen rather than a Mary sitting at His feet.

So I've started a new practice: intentional cancellation. That might mean I drop an evening meeting to have game night with my kids. Or I decline a speaking invite because my soul needs a weekend off. Rather than feeling guilt, I remind myself that every "yes" and "no" should come from listening to God.

If I never ask Him, "Lord, is this what You want me to do?" I'll end up overloaded by even good activities. These days, I periodically scan my calendar and prayerfully ask, "What can go?" It's incredible how the world keeps spinning when I do this and how my awareness of God's presence increases. In the margin, I can hear His voice more clearly. In the white space of a blank evening, I might finally pour out that prayer or open my Bible without rushing.

Maybe you're like me, a recovering over-committer. If so, this is your permission to hit the pause button. Cancel a little chaos. It's okay. You're not the Savior of the world. You belong to Him. And He'd much rather have your attentive heart than your frantic sacrifice. *God can do more through a rested, surrendered you than through an exhausted, control freak you. I'm living proof. Let's be still and watch Him be God.* He's really good at it.

Reflection Questions

- Have you ever reached a point of burnout or near breakdown from an overloaded schedule? What led up to it, and what signals might God have been sending you along the way to slow down?
- What is one commitment or activity you sense you may need to step back from or cancel, at least for a season? Pray about this and listen for God's guidance.
- When you think about being still or resting, what fears arise? How does trusting God's sovereignty address those fears and enable you to rest in His provision?

Sunday 23:

The Veil Is Torn

I want to know Christ—yes, to know the power
of his resurrection and participation in his
sufferings, becoming like him in his death.
—PHILIPPIANS 3:10

BEFORE ENDURING THE cross, Jesus gave us example after example of lavish love. He washed the feet of Judas, the very one who would betray Him. Hanging in agony on the cross, He still paused to extend mercy to a criminal who begged to be remembered. This is love extravagantly poured out; love that costs something. And here's the mystery: In those hardest, most sacrificial moments, the presence of God was palpably near. The veil thinned. Heaven touched earth.

I see a glimpse of this in our Isaiah 117 Houses. Some of the situations we encounter are gut-wrenchingly hard, with children arriving with bruises you can see and trauma you can't. Our volunteers get tired and sometimes discouraged. Yet, when they press through and love "one more time" even though they're spent, there's this holy moment where God's presence floods the room.

I've often felt that when we dig deep to love a child in the midnight hour, or forgive someone who's wronged us, or serve when it hurts, it's like the veil between us and God becomes tissue thin. You tangibly sense "God is with us."

Why? I think it's because that's where Jesus is. He's right in the midst of the pain and the mess, doing what He does and loving lavishly. When we join Him there, we experience His heart like never before. It reminds me of Philippians 3:10 where Paul says, "I want to know Christ—yes, to know the power of his resurrection and participation in his sufferings, becoming like him in his death."

There's an intimacy with Jesus that we discover when we're willing to stay in the hard place and love anyway. Every foster parent who's loved a child fiercely only to say goodbye later knows this. Every spouse who has loved through a long illness, every friend who has stuck by another through addiction or relapse—they all attest that God felt particularly close in those seasons. It's not that He isn't with us in the easy times. It's that we often become most aware of Him in the fire of sacrifice.

I realized through my tears in church that I often want resurrection power without cruciform love. I pray, "Lord, use me," but shy away when it requires costly love. A love that forgives the betrayer, washes the feet of one who's hurt me, or expends energy on someone unlikely to repay it. But that is precisely the kind of love that rips veils and opens the way for God's kingdom to break through. It's love that looks like Jesus.

So I challenge you this week not to run from the hard. Don't hold back when it's painful. That's when your love looks most like Christ's. And that's when people don't just hear about Jesus, they see Him.

Reflection Questions

- Identify one relationship or situation where you've been hesitant to "lavishly love" because it's costly or painful. What would Christlike love look like in that context?
- When have you felt God's presence most strongly in your life? Was it during a time of comfortable ease or in the midst of a sacrificial act of love or suffering?

- Pray about any "veils" in your heart and ask God to gently tear those veils and fill you with His love, even for those who are hard to love. What step of lavish love can you take this week, trusting God to meet you there?

Look for "the Least of These"

*Truly I tell you, whatever you did for one of the least
of these brothers and sisters of mine, you did for me.*
—MATTHEW 25:40

I HAVE TO SMILE when I think about how this ministry journey often has me zooming around the country, fueled by coffee and true crime podcasts, visiting people in every corner. It's exciting, and a little scary sometimes (Yes, I do check my back seat at gas stations!). But in all my travels, one question keeps tugging at my heart: Am I truly loving "the least of these" who Jesus talks about?

I share the mission of Isaiah 117 House everywhere, and people nod along because we all know Christ calls us to love the most vulnerable. Yet, a hard truth hit me: In my comfortable daily routine, I barely see those who might be considered "least." My friends largely look and live like I do. My neighbors are doing fine. My church circle is healthy and happy. If I'm honest, it's possible for me to sail through most days without ever rubbing shoulders with someone who's hungry, or homeless, or struggling. And how can I feed the hungry or clothe the naked if I never actually encounter them?

Jesus's words in Scripture challenge me here: "Truly I tell you, whatever you did for one of the least of these brothers and sisters of mine, you did for me." That means every act of love to someone in need is love offered to Jesus Himself. But first I have to get near those needs.

So I've been asking God to open my eyes and maybe nudge me out of my comfort zone. The easy path for me is to stick with people who are just like me. Yet Jesus intentionally sought out the hurting and the marginalized. He dined with those others ignored and noticed those others avoided. If I want to follow Him, I suspect I'll have to step into some unfamiliar places and relationships.

This week, challenge yourself to find the courage to step out of your comfort zone. Don't overlook the coworker who seems down. Ask if they're okay and truly listen. Instead of just waving at the single mom on your street, consider inviting her for coffee and opening your heart to her story. Make an effort to start a conversation with the elderly man eating alone after church. These small actions can break you out of your bubble and connect you to someone else's world.

Look around for those who might be "least" in the world's eyes and intentionally connect with them. It might mean volunteering at a shelter or simply noticing the quiet student at the edge of your friend group and reaching out. Jesus promised that as we care for them, we are actually caring for Him. What an honor and adventure that is!

Reflection Questions

- In your daily routines, are you encountering people who might be among "the least of these"? If not, what could you change to see and engage with them more?
- Think of one person or group in your community who is often overlooked or in need. How might you step out of your comfort zone this week to show them Christlike love?
- When you feel hesitant to reach out to those who are different or struggling, what practical steps can help you overcome that fear?

Fall in Love with God

*Love the Lord your God with all your heart and with all
your soul and with all your mind and with all your strength.*
—MARK 12:30

A WHILE AGO, I was crazy nervous about an important meeting for our foster care ministry. I prayed and talked and prayed some more as we prepared to meet a state official. And God showed up. The meeting went even better than expected. As I walked along the shoreline afterward, heart soaring with gratitude, I realized somewhere in that busy season I'd fallen head over heels in love with God.

Now, I've been a Christian for a long time. But what I'm experiencing lately feels new and vibrant. It's like when I first fell in love with my husband, Corey. I remember the early days of getting to know him and finding out he was not just cute but also hilarious and smart. I treasured every conversation and text message. Over time, those little interactions built a deep trust and love between us.

That's exactly what's happening between God and me. As I spend constant, daily time with Him—chatting in the car, whispering prayers of thanks, asking for help in the moment—I realize I'm in an ongoing conversation with the God of the universe. And amazingly, He wants that connection with me! Little old me, with sand in my toes and a million flaws, is loved by a God who actually longs to hear my voice.

If that doesn't warm your heart, I don't know what will. It blows my mind that our infinite God desires a personal relationship with each of us. No appointment needed, no "I'll get back to you later." As the Apostle Paul encourages in 1 Thessalonians 5:17, you can "pray continually," keeping an open line with God all day, in every situation. And you know what happens when you do? You start noticing Him everywhere.

I find myself sharing every joy, fear, and goofy thought with Jesus as natural as breathing. He's not a distant deity in a stained glass window. He's my dearest friend. The more I open up to Him, the more I sense His gentle guidance and overwhelming love. It's a two-way street. I draw near to Him and He draws near to me.

If you feel intimidated by the idea of "loving God" or wonder how to deepen your relationship with Him, take heart. It's not about mustering up emotional feelings or performing perfectly. It's about time. Just like any friendship, love grows with time and attention. Start with simple conversations.

This week, tell God what's on your mind during your morning commute. Thank Him for one small blessing before bed. Read a bit of His Word and ask Him what He wants you to see. Over time, those little moments string together into a beautiful relationship. Before you know it, you'll realize your day feels incomplete without chatting with Jesus. You'll crave that connection.

Reflection Questions

- What would it look like for you to include God in the little moments of your day? Identify one routine where you can start a conversation with Him.
- Think of a human friendship you enjoy that has grown deeper over time. What priorities and practices have encouraged that relationship to flourish? How can you

apply those principles to your relationship with God this week?

- If talking to God feels awkward, try writing a short prayer in a journal or singing along to a worship song. What do you notice as you intentionally connect with Him each day?

Summer

Grateful

*Come with me by yourselves to a quiet place
and get some rest.*
—Mark 6:31

I'M CONSTANTLY REMINDED by books, articles, and podcasts of my need to slow down in this crazy digital age. Recently, I was reading a John Eldredge book titled *Get Your Life Back*, and it opened my eyes to how relentlessly I can rush from one thing to the next. One moment, I'm calming an anxious child, and the next, I'm on a tense call with the insurance company. Then I'm juggling back-to-back meetings, emails, and family needs without a moment to breathe.

No wonder I sometimes feel drained and distant from God! The author pointed out that not long ago, life had natural pauses. There were quiet drives between appointments, gaps with no incoming emails or news, even moments of boredom. Now, every spare second gets filled with stimulation or tasks. Our souls have zero transition time, zero time to reset.

Jesus, on the other hand, modeled a better rhythm. In Scripture we see that, even in the middle of His urgent mission, He never lived in constant rush. After big, miraculous moments, He would step away to be alone and to pray, while His disciples processed what had happened while strolling on the way to the next town. Jesus built in transitions, giving everyone time to reflect and rest. If the Son of God needed those pauses, surely we do too!

That realization struck a chord in me as it's actually at the heart of what our Isaiah 117 House ministry provides: a sacred pause for children in crisis. When kids are removed from their homes, they shouldn't have to go from one really hard, confusing state to another really hard, confusing time without respite. So our homes create a moment of peace to take a breath, to hurt and cry and think before going on to the next place.

Thinking about transitions made me deeply grateful for the fifteen-thousand-plus children to which we've been able to give that gift of rest. I found myself thanking God for every supporter who helps create those breathing spaces. Today, I'm taking that lesson personally. I want to embrace the little pauses God offers each day, like putting down my phone on the drive home, sitting in silence for a few minutes, stepping outside to pray between emails.

Instead of cramming every second with stimulation, I choose to allow margin for my soul to catch up. I'm discovering that when I honor those transitions, I actually notice God's presence so much more. He was there all along, waiting for my racing mind to slow down enough to meet him.

This week, you don't have to be enslaved to the hectic pace of this world. You can choose a better way—a grateful, restful way. And you can trust that God will meet you in the quiet moments you carve out.

Reflection Questions

- Where can you create small "transition" moments in your day to pause, breathe, and refocus on God?
- What activities or habits might you cut back on this summer to allow your soul some breathing room?
- How have you experienced God's presence when you intentionally slowed down or rested? What might He be saying to you in the quiet?

Sabbath Delight

*Six days you shall labor, but on the seventh
day you shall rest; even during the plowing
season and harvest you must rest.*
—Exodus 34:21

STILL REMEMBER THAT one Fourth of July where my family spent the day lazily out at a friend's lake house, doing nothing in particular. As dusk fell, the neighbors launched a spectacular fireworks show over the water. My kids literally bobbed in the lake with life jackets, fireworks exploding right above their heads. They had no idea how lucky they were!

On the ride home, I found myself chuckling like a nostalgic mom. "You don't understand," I told them. "Normal people have to load the car, drive for hours, sit in a hot parking lot to maybe see fireworks in the distance, then battle traffic afterward. But you guys got to splash in the lake, then simply look up and enjoy the show!" They didn't grasp the big deal because to them, it was just a fun day with family and friends, capped off by sparkles in the sky. But to me, it was a vivid picture of sabbath delight.

That day on the lake felt like what God intended the Sabbath to be: a gift of rest and joy amid our busy lives. We had nowhere else to be and nothing we had to get done. We literally played, relaxed, watched fireworks, and just were. In our modern hustle culture, such unhurried togetherness is rare. Yet God commanded His people to enjoy exactly that rhythm once a week.

He said in Exodus 34:21, "Six days you shall labor, but on the seventh day you shall rest; even during the plowing season and harvest you must rest." I love that He added "and harvest you must rest," meaning even when there's more work to do than hours in the day, God still calls us to stop and rest. That shows how serious He is about the Sabbath.

Now, I'll admit I haven't always honored the Sabbath. It's so tempting to treat Sunday like any other catch-up day. But this past year, my family has been on a journey to reclaim sabbath delight. No agenda, no rushing, and a whole lot of lingering in the moment.

I've learned two big things through practicing sabbath. First, God can do more with my six days of work than I can with seven. When I trust Him enough to pause, He provides. Second, the Sabbath is supposed to be fun! It's not about legalistic rules; it's about reconnecting with God and the people you love. Jesus said, "The Sabbath was made for man, not man for the Sabbath" (Mark 2:27). It's God's gift to us, a day to recharge our bodies and rejoice in our blessings—like giggling kids, sparkling fireworks, and long summer afternoons with nowhere to be.

This week, God invites you to unwrap the gift of sabbath. So dare to set aside your to-do lists for one day and embrace holy rest. Fire up the grill, lounge in a hammock, worship freely, watch a sunset. Trust that your work can wait, because your soul cannot.

Reflection Questions

- What would a truly restful, joyful Sabbath day look like for you? Brainstorm a few activities that draw you closer to God and replenish you.
- What challenges or excuses usually keep you from resting on the Sabbath? How can you address those and trust God with your time?
- This week, plan one "sabbath-like" period where you step away from work, chores, and screens.

Trusting God with Our Children

Pour out your hearts to him, for God is our refuge.
—Psalm 62:8

NOTHING MAKES A mama's heart beat like knowing your daughter just got engaged. When I first heard the news, I was over the moon. But can I confess something? Ever since my kids were little, I fretted about their future spouses. I'd rock my baby girl and half-jokingly pray, "Lord, someday let her marry someone who loves You (and maybe loves us too!)."

As she grew, those what-if worries occasionally crept in. What if she marries somebody we don't like? What if he's not good to her or doesn't share her faith? Through every teenage crush of hers, I'd be silently grilling the poor boy in my mind. Does he treat her kindly? Does he respect her values? Okay, maybe I was more than a little protective.

Fast-forward to when a nervous young man stood beside my husband in the ocean, asking for his blessing to propose. I almost laughed with joy and relief. This was the very scenario I had prayed for and worried about! Here before me was a godly, kind-hearted fella who not only adores my daughter but also loves Jesus. I thought about all those years of mom-anxiety. Why did I waste so much energy fearing the worst when God was working out the best? It's as if God gently nudged me, saying, "See, I had her in My hands all along."

Now, I know life isn't a Hallmark movie. Sometimes our prayers for our kids seem unanswered for a long time. Maybe you raised your child in church, and they're now far from God. Maybe marriage or grandbabies haven't come as you hoped. Trust me, I have other prayers for my kids I'm still waiting on. But my daughter's engagement reminded me that God hears a parent's prayers. Through every worried whisper I poured out about her future, He was listening. And in His timing, He answered in a beautiful way.

This journey has taught me God loves my children even more than I do. When I stay up late concerned for their tomorrows, He's already there in their tomorrows, working for their good. My job is to pray and trust. I'm learning to exchange hand-wringing for knee-bending and choosing prayer over panic.

So if you're a parent anxiously watching your child navigate life, take heart. Keep praying faithfully for them this week. Entrust them to the One who crafted them in the womb and has a perfect plan for their life. There might be twists and turns, but God is not caught off guard. Go ahead, pour out your heart for your children to God. And then rest, knowing He is a safe refuge for them and for you. He hears. He cares. And he's still in the business of answering a mama's prayers.

Reflection Questions

- What is one worry or fear you consistently have about your child's future? Have you explicitly given that concern over to God in prayer?
- Think of a time you saw a prayer for someone you love answered in an unexpected or wonderful way. How does remembering that instance build your faith for other areas still in progress?
- In what practical ways can you "pour out your heart" to God on behalf of your family? How might this practice help replace your anxiety with peace?

Be Known for Love

*By this everyone will know that you are
my disciples, if you love one another.*
—John 13:35

NOT LONG AGO, I found myself standing in a brand-new Isaiah 117 House in Georgia, about to cut the ribbon for its grand opening. As I marveled at the beautiful home, I felt overwhelmed by the goodness of God and the goodness of His people. Every time we expand into a new area, I ask, "Why has this movement spread so fast?"

Yes, the need is huge and God is huge, but there's something more. God's people rally when love is the focus. In these little white houses with red doors, believers from all backgrounds come together to love children in crisis. We're not bickering over worship styles or carpet colors. We're united in what matters, being the hands and feet of Jesus for "the least of these."

It reminded me of a powerful encouragement from the book of Titus I had read recently. In a tiny passage often overlooked, Paul essentially pleads: "Christians, please don't be known for arguing and quarreling. Be known for being good. Be known for love!"

Y'all, there's some nuggets in Titus, because that hit me so hard. The Scripture literally says not to be known for quarreling or bickering, but "to be peaceable and considerate, and always to be gentle toward everyone" (Titus 3:2). It's a call for God's people to rise above pettiness and showcase love.

I need that reminder often. It's easy, especially in the age of social media, to slip into debate mode or to divide over minor differences. But God's Word calls us to a higher standard. Jesus said the world will know we are His disciples by our love for one another, not by our snappy comebacks or perfectly argued theology. Love doesn't mean we never speak truth; it does mean we keep kindness, compassion, and humility at the forefront.

In a world increasingly marked by outrage and division, you and I have an opportunity to shine by doing the opposite. Imagine if people described Christians as "those folks who are always doing good, always kind, always loving." That's my prayer.

So this week, let's start with the small stuff. Let's hold our tongue when we're tempted to snap, assuming the best in others, serving without seeking credit. Over time, those choices add up to a reputation. May ours be a reputation of love.

Reflection Questions

- Take a moment to evaluate what you're "known for" among your family, friends, and coworkers. Would people say that you are more often loving and kind, or critical and argumentative?
- Think of a recent disagreement or tense situation you were in. How could focusing on being loving have changed the outcome or atmosphere?
- Who is someone in your life who needs to experience the love of Christ through you this week? What's one concrete way you can show them kindness or goodness?

We Can't Take the Easy Way Out

Dear children, let us not love with words or
speech but with actions and in truth.
—1 John 3:18

I HAVE A CONFESSION. When I'm exhausted, I look for shortcuts everywhere. During a back-to-school week a few years ago, I was bone-tired. One evening my husband, Corey, glanced at me and asked, "Do you feel ragged?" I just nodded.

In that worn-down state, I caught myself slacking as a mom, handing my kid a device to avoid a meltdown, letting chores slide, considering pizza delivery for the third night in a row. I wanted the easiest way out of every hard thing! And you know what? It backfired. Giving my child extra screen time made him crankier. Avoiding a tough conversation with my spouse only caused more tension later. Even all that Papa John's left us with heartburn and regrets.

That week, God gently opened my eyes. There is no "easy button" for the important stuff in life. In fact, taking the easy way out often creates bigger problems. Nowhere is this truer than in our faith. I realized sometimes we Christians reduce Jesus's message to a catchy slogan like "Love God, love people" and pat ourselves on the back as if quoting it is enough.

And it's true! Jesus *did* boil the commandments down to loving God and others. But actually living that out? That's the hard part. Loving God and loving people is hard, because sometimes people stink. It's messy to truly love others, to forgive when you've been hurt, to be patient with difficult personalities, to sacrifice your comfort to meet someone else's need. It's anything but easy.

It's one thing to say, "Yes, we should care for orphans," but quite another to welcome a traumatized child into your home 24/7. When my husband and I became foster parents and eventually adopted, we learned a lot. Late-night tantrums, therapy appointments, and endless forms sapped our energy. Loving a child from a hard place demanded that we die to ourselves daily. But it also brought the greatest blessings and joy that "easy" never could.

The early Christians had a reputation for extraordinary love. They didn't just preach slogans; they showed up for people by caring for outcasts, rescuing abandoned babies, sharing all they had. I want my faith to be like that. I don't want to take the convenient shortcuts of just posting Bible verses on Facebook or sticking a bumper sticker on my car, yet never actually doing anything.

So next time you're tempted this week to spiritually "phone it in," remember that the easy way isn't really easy in the end. Choose the higher, harder road of love in action. It might cost you something now, but you will meet Jesus there. And He will bless you in ways you could never imagine.

Reflection Questions

- In what areas of your faith have you been taking the easy way out?
- Identify one person in your life who is difficult to love. What is a concrete way you can show them love this week, even if it's hard or inconvenient?
- Jesus accepted and loved you at your worst. How might remembering His grace toward you help you choose the harder path of actively loving someone else?

Silence and Solitude

Be still, and know that I am God.
—PSALM 46:10

IF YOU HAD told me years ago that I'd voluntarily spend forty-eight hours completely alone in silence, with no phone, no TV, no people, and not even my dog, I would've laughed. I'm an extroverted, busy mom of four. The idea of being by myself with nothing to do sounded either impossible or insane. But this is what I set out to do.

It all started when I felt God nudging me to go on a personal retreat. Our organization gives staff a day in the spring and fall for a spiritual retreat, and I decided to take it a step further with two full days of silence and solitude at a little cabin. No agenda except to rest and be with Jesus. Let me tell you, leading up to it, I was nervous. I packed my Bible and journal, but I also packed about five other books "just in case" I got bored.

I kept telling my friends, "I don't know how I feel about this, because the thought of that much quiet gives me butterflies." It truly did. The same butterflies I used to get before a track meet in high school!

When I arrived at the cabin, the first few hours were the hardest. My thoughts were racing with all the things I'd been too busy to process. It took a while to detox from the constant noise of life. But after a good night's sleep and some time journaling my worries out to

God, I began to settle in. I took a slow hike in the woods and noticed things I'd normally speed past—the crunch of leaves under my feet, the chorus of birds overhead, the intricate pattern of a wildflower.

I prayed out loud and sang a little. I even took a nap without setting an alarm! As the hours passed, an unexpected peace washed over me. I realized God was there with me in the silence, and He'd been waiting for me to get quiet enough to notice.

In those two days, I didn't have any dramatic visions or write a bestselling manifesto. What I did have were gentle yet powerful encounters with the Lord. Certain Scriptures I read seemed to leap off the page as personal messages. Old memories surfaced, and I invited Jesus into those hurts for healing. I cried some cleansing tears. I laughed out loud at one point, realizing how overcomplicated I make things. Mostly, I felt God's presence tenderly near, and I came home with a soul that felt lighter, like I'd been truly seen and heard by my Father.

One thing God reminded me of during this retreat is that He longs to spend time with us, but we rarely slow down enough to give Him that time. Obviously, I can't do forty-eight hours every week, but I can carve out smaller pockets of silence and solitude. I set a fifteen-minute timer and light a candle some mornings, signaling my brain it's quiet time with Jesus.

If the idea of being alone with God scares you a little, you're not weird. It just means it's probably exactly what you need. Start small this week, if you must, but start. Turn off the noise and let your soul breathe. Your Father is waiting to meet you in the secret place.

Reflection Questions

- Making space for silence can be challenging but rewarding. What steps could you take to reduce that noise, even for a short time, each day?
- How does the idea of spending time in solitude with God make you feel? Talk to God honestly about those feelings.

- Plan a mini "solitude retreat" for yourself. It could be a few hours or a day. Where could you go and what ground rules will you set? What do you hope God will do in your heart during that time?

Scars Make Us Who We Are

*But he was pierced for our transgressions, he was crushed
for our iniquities; the punishment that brought us
peace was on him, and by his wounds we are healed.*
—Isaiah 53:5

NOT LONG AGO, I found myself on the injured reserve list for something you wouldn't expect at my age: kickball. Yes, at fifty years old, I agreed to play in an adult kickball birthday party! As I rounded third base, I heard a loud pop. My hamstring tore completely off the bone, and before I knew it, I was headed into surgery.

Now, if the injury had ended there, it would've been bad enough. But the complications kept coming. Six weeks into recovery, my incision looked a little infected. As I was applying ointment one day, it burst wide open. My squeamish husband panicked, and off we rushed to the doctor. For weeks after that, I leaked like a slug (my affectionate nickname for myself during that season). The wound just wouldn't close. Even after a second surgery and stitches, I had an allergic reaction to the nylon, and the whole ordeal dragged on.

Through all of it, I learned something surprising about scars. From the beginning, I was told to rub vitamin E oil on my incision so the scar would stay soft and less noticeable. I followed that advice faithfully. But I started to wonder if, in trying to minimize the scar, I was keeping it from doing what it was meant to do. A scar's job is to knit skin back together, to hold things in place, to remind you that healing has occurred. Sometimes the very thing we try hardest to erase is the thing God intends for our good.

I see this truth in people's stories too. When I ask folks, "What's one thing in your life you wish you could change?" many share a painful chapter. Yet more often than not, they end by saying, "I don't think I'd actually change it." Why? Because those hard seasons, those scars, brought them closer to Jesus. The very pain they'd never have chosen made them who they are.

Scripture points us to the same lesson. When Thomas doubted the resurrection, Jesus invited him to touch His scars. The proof of His suffering was also the proof of His identity. Without the wounds, Thomas may never have believed. And Isaiah reminds us that it's by Jesus's wounds, His scars, that we are healed. Our Savior did not hide His scars. He showed them as a testimony of love and redemption.

We try so hard to avoid pain, but Jesus told us to take up our cross daily. That means we will face hurt. Pain leads to wounds. Wounds lead to scars. And scars, when we allow God to use them, can make us more like Christ.

So here's my encouragement for you this week. Don't despise your scars. Don't hide them or wish them away. Let them be reminders that you endured, that you healed, and that God met you in the middle of it all. My own scar will always remind me to slow down, literally sit myself down, and spend more time with Jesus. I don't know what your scars remind you of, but I hope they point you back to Him.

Reflection Questions

- Can you think of a "scar" in your life—physical, emotional, or spiritual—that shaped who you are today? How has God used it for your good?

- Why do you think Jesus chose to keep His scars after the resurrection (John 20:24–28)? What does that teach us about the redemptive purpose of scars in our lives?
- What painful season are you walking through now that may one day become a scar? How might you begin to look for Jesus in the middle of your circumstances instead of only wishing the pain away?

Enough for Today

*The people are to go out each day
and gather enough for that day.*
—Exodus 16:4

WHEN I LEFT my stable, beloved job of thirteen years to step fully into leading Isaiah 117 House ministry, I was excited but also terrified. All the "what if" questions swarmed my mind. *What if the ministry funding dries up in a few years? What if I can't handle the pressure? How will we afford college for the kids now without my employee tuition benefit?* In the midst of my anxiety, God drew my attention to an Old Testament story and a single word that became my anchor: ENOUGH.

The story was Israel in the wilderness, when God provided manna, the mysterious bread from heaven. Each morning, the Israelites would wake up to find the ground covered in what looked like thin flakes of frost. They could collect it and bake it into bread to eat. But they could only gather enough for that day. If they tried to stockpile manna for the next day, it rotted. God was very deliberate about this daily rhythm. Through this, God taught His people to trust Him one day at a time. He literally built reliance into their routine.

In those days during my job transition, I felt like one of those Israelites, stepping into unknown territory, having to trust God for provisions I couldn't yet see. In my journal I wrote, "Lord, I have no idea how the future will unfold, but You promise I'll have enough for today. Help me learn to lean on You daily." I kept coming back to that. When anxiety about next month or next year flared up, I sensed Him whisper, "Am I providing for you today? Then be at peace. I will provide tomorrow when it comes." It's exactly what Jesus taught: "Do not worry about tomorrow . . . Each day has enough trouble of its own" (Matthew 6:34). In other words, handle today with God; let Him handle tomorrow.

Are you at the end of your rope? You might feel utterly spent and wonder how you'll face another day. Hear this: God will give you enough for today. And when tomorrow becomes today, He'll give you enough for that day too.

One of God's names in the Bible is Jehovah Jireh, meaning "the Lord will provide." I've come to love that name. It doesn't mean He gives us everything we want (He's not Jehovah Genie!). But like a good father, He provides what we need when we need it. Sometimes just in the nick of time. The manna fell each morning, not a week's supply at once.

In my journey, I've seen God do this over and over. Funding for our nonprofit appears right when a big bill is due. Strength or wisdom bubbles up right when I'm about to give out. An encouraging text from a friend pings exactly when I'm battling despair. These are not coincidences; they are manna. They are daily bread from a God who sees me.

Trusting God daily can be harder than hoarding. Hoarding feels like control, while daily trust feels vulnerable. But daily trust builds relationship. It keeps us coming back to God each morning, saying, "Okay, Lord, I'm here for my manna. I trust You for what I need today." That's a prayer I challenge you to pray each day this week.

Reflection Questions

- It's time to exchange our worries for trust in Jehovah Jireh. What are your biggest "what if" worries about the future? Write them down, then prayerfully surrender each one to God.

- Think of a time in the past when you weren't sure how a situation would work out, but in hindsight you see that God provided what you needed. How does remembering that past faithfulness encourage you to trust Him now?
- Each morning this week, pause and pray, "Lord, give me today my daily bread, and the grace, strength, and provision I need for these next twenty-four hours."

The Father's Heart

*See what great love the Father has lavished on
us, that we should be called children of God!*
—1 JOHN 3:1

WHEN YOU THINK of "God the Father," there's a chance the word "Father" might not bring up warm feelings for you. If so, I am truly sorry. People can fail us so profoundly, and when it's a parent, the wounds cut especially deep.

But know this, your heavenly Father loves you and He is pursuing you and wants to work all things out for your good. This is the core message of the Bible. God describes Himself as a father to the fatherless, a defender of the weak. Jesus taught us to address God as "our Father," and depicted Him as the dad who runs to embrace his wayward child in the story of the prodigal son (Luke 15:11–32).

For me, this truth became real through our experiences with foster care and adoption. I've seen children who have been neglected or hurt by earthly parents gradually learn to trust and love again in the care of a healthy family. One teenager who came into our home had been through unthinkable trauma. She understandably kept her walls high at first. But we just kept showing up for her by providing meals, helping with homework, and listening without judgment.

Over time, consistency and unconditional love broke through her defenses. She realized we weren't going to abandon her, even when she pushed back. If flawed humans like us can show that kind of steadfast love, how much more is God capable of loving us perfectly!

In fact, any good we see in human parents is just a dim reflection of His goodness. Conversely, the failures of human parents are not a reflection of Him at all. He is the sole standard of fatherhood. For every time your dad or mom fell short, God stands ready to exceed your hopes. Where your father was angry, God is patient. Where your father was absent, God is intimately present. Where your father's love had limits or conditions, God's love never fails and never gives up on you.

One of my favorite verses is Psalm 27:10: "Though my father and mother forsake me, the LORD will receive me." This tells me that even if the people who should care for us most deeply don't come through, God is right there to scoop us up. He says, "I'll be your Father. I'll take you in."

So if you carry a father wound, I gently challenge you this week not to project that hurt onto God. Instead, let God Himself begin to heal it. It might be through counseling, or through other father figures and mentor relationships, or directly through experiencing His presence in prayer. You don't have to perform or earn His affection. He loves you as you are.

Reflection Questions

- How have your experiences with your earthly parents (good or bad) shaped how you view God?
- What Scriptures or stories from Jesus's life show you what God the Father is really like?
- If viewing God as a loving Father is hard for you, consider taking a step toward healing by perhaps writing a letter to God about your feelings, talking to a pastor or counselor, or simply praying, "God, show me Your Father heart." What might be a first step for you?

Go and Do Likewise

"Love the Lord your God with all your heart and with all your soul and with all your strength and with all your mind"; and, "Love your neighbor as yourself."
—LUKE 10:27

I THOUGHT I KNEW the parable of the Good Samaritan inside and out. I've taught it to kids for years and heard countless sermons on it. But one Sunday morning it hit me in a new way. At church, we read Jesus's story in Luke 10 about the beaten man lying on the roadside and the three passersby.

For once, I found myself less focused on the heroic Samaritan and more on the two religious men who did nothing. A priest saw the injured man and literally crossed to the other side of the road to avoid him. Then a Levite (another supposedly godly man) did the same. They just kept walking. It was the outsider, the Samaritan—someone looked down on in that culture—who stopped and helped the wounded stranger.

As I sat there, a convicting question formed, and I thought, *Am I ever like that priest or Levite?* They probably had important temple business and were in a hurry. Maybe they felt sad for the victim but told themselves someone else would help. Whatever their excuses, Jesus doesn't sugarcoat it. They failed to show love when it mattered. And I realized this parable is a mirror for believers today.

The world is watching Christians closely, and people are looking to see if our actions line up with what we preach. When we come across someone in need, do we respond with compassionate action, or do we avert our eyes and pass by on the other side?

What struck me next was how far the Samaritan went to help. He didn't just do the bare minimum. He stopped his journey, tended the man's wounds with oil and wine, lifted him onto his own donkey, and brought him to an inn to take care of him.

The next day, he paid the innkeeper out of his own pocket and even promised to come back later to cover any extra expenses. This wasn't convenient or cheap for him, but he did it anyway. The Samaritan had every social reason to ignore this Jewish man, yet he showed extravagant mercy. Jesus said the Samaritan was the true neighbor to the man in need, and His command was, "Go and do likewise."

I left church thinking about how often *I* fail to "go and do likewise." I don't want to be someone who talks about loving others but then ignores the hurting person right in front of me.

This week, as you go about your routine, keep your eyes open for the "neighbors" God places in your path. It might be a colleague having a hard day, a homeless person on the corner, or even a family member who needs extra grace. Don't overthink whether they deserve help or whether you have time. Just stop and show mercy.

Be the one who stops when others keep going. If we all live out this kind of practical love, people will see Jesus through us without us ever having to hear a sermon. Let's be the Good Samaritan in a world full of bypassers.

Reflection Questions

- Jesus praised the Samaritan who stopped to help. Who are the people you tend to "pass by" or avoid? Why do you think that is?
- Can you recall a time when you were in need, and someone unexpectedly helped you? How did that change your perspective on loving your neighbor?

- What is one concrete way you can show mercy to a stranger or someone outside your usual circle this week? Think of a need you can meet, even if it's inconvenient.

No Applause Needed

*So you also, when you have done everything you
were told to do, should say, "We are unworthy
servants; we have only done our duty."*
—LUKE 17:10

A WHILE BACK, SOMEONE nominated me as a "community hero" in our town. When I got the news, I honestly felt awkward. *Me? A hero?* Sure, it came with a nice write-up in the paper, and I'm thankful it brought attention to Isaiah 117 House, but having cameras in my face and people calling me a hero felt surreal and undeserved. My close friends and family had a field day teasing me about it, texting, "Hey, community hero!" with all the laughing emojis. If my head ever started to swell, trust me, they popped it real quick.

The very next night after the community hero spotlight appeared in the paper, I was asked to pray the invocation at a big race at Bristol Motor Speedway. I was told I might be the first woman ever to do that at this event. Talk about pressure! People often ask if I get nervous speaking in public. Usually I'm fine, but this time I had butterflies.

They gave me a strict thirty-second window to pray before the race. Do you know how hard it is to fit anything meaningful into thirty seconds? I had written out a short prayer, but when I timed myself at home, it was a minute and a half! By the time I stood on that start-finish line, I was sweating bullets. But by God's grace, I got through it. It was an amazing night and truly an honor.

I share these two experiences not to toot my own horn but to make a point. After the race and the "hero" article, several people said to me, "It's so inspiring that you just did what God asked you to do. Thank you for your obedience." They meant well, and I appreciate the encouragement. But something about that kept tugging at me. Why should it be *inspiring* that a Christian actually followed what God put on their heart? Isn't that what we're all supposed to do, every day?

I'm not special or super-spiritual. I'm literally just trying to follow Jesus, same as any believer. If God calls me to love foster kids or pray in public or help someone in need, I want my response to be as natural as breathing: *Of course I'll do it.*

Somehow, we've started treating basic Christian love and service like it's headline news, when really it should be the norm. The real story should be when Christians *don't* step up to love others, because that's actually more shocking. Jesus already told us clearly what to do. We're to feed the hungry, welcome the stranger, care for the orphan and widow, love your neighbor, even love your enemies. It's not complicated, just hard.

He never said, "Do these things so you'll get awards and applause." He said, "Do them because this is how my Father loves you, and I want you to love others the same way."

What if we Christians had that same attitude? Imagine quietly serving others and not needing to post about it or get a pat on the back. What if loving people in Jesus's name was so normal for us that we didn't think it deserved a celebration?

This week, as you find opportunities to do good, try doing it for an audience of One. Love that difficult person, help someone in need, go out of your way to show kindness, and then don't tell a soul. Do it simply because it's who you are in Christ. You may feel invisible or unappreciated at times, but remember, God sees every act of love done in His name. And in the end, His "well done" is the only praise that matters.

Reflection Questions

- Do you ever crave recognition or thanks when you serve or give to others? How can you remind yourself that serving is simply part of your calling as a Christian?
- Think of a humble person you know who always helps others behind the scenes. What have you learned from their example, and how can you emulate their humility this week?
- What is one way you can "do good in secret" this week? Consider a kind act you can perform without anyone besides God knowing.

Are You and God Good?

Therefore, since we have been justified through faith, we have peace with God through our Lord Jesus Christ.
—ROMANS 5:1

NOT LONG AGO, my son's sweet girlfriend looked at me and remarked, "Ronda, you seem so peaceful and like you're really okay." I paused, smiled, and replied with a phrase that summed up years of journey: "Me and God are good."

I realized as I said it that it was true. Like deep-in-my-bones true. But it hadn't always been that way. I spent a lot of my life secretly worrying that God was disappointed in me. I'm a classic overachiever and recovering people pleaser, so I tended to project that onto my relationship with God. I figured, sure, He loves me in a salvation sense, but does He like me? Probably not when I'm messing up. So I better work really hard to stay on His good side.

That mindset led me to be quite the busy Christian bee. Volunteering for everything, saying yes to everyone, never admitting my limits. On the outside, I looked like a model believer. On the inside, I was exhausted and anxious, afraid to slow down in case I might let God down. It's ironic, because Jesus literally said, "My yoke is easy and my burden is light" (Matthew 11:30), but I was lugging around a five-hundred-pound backpack of religious guilt and duty!

Eventually, something had to give. In my case it was a mini-breakdown in a McDonald's parking lot (as I've shared before) that forced me to seek help and embrace rest. That was the beginning of relearning who I am to God. Through counseling, prayer, and saturating myself in Scriptures about God's love, I gradually internalized a life-changing truth that God isn't waiting for me to earn His love; I already have it. Like, right now, as I am.

He actually enjoys me. Zephaniah 3:17 says He sings over us with delight! When I first heard that, I honestly thought, "Maybe over other people, but not me." I had to let the Holy Spirit rewire that faulty thinking. One tender step at a time, He did.

I remember a specific moment sitting on my porch, Bible in lap, reading Romans 5:8: "But God demonstrates His own love for us in this: While we were still sinners, Christ died for us." I'd read it a hundred times, but that day it clicked. Christ didn't die for a polished-up, super-spiritual version of me; He died for the messy, real me.

The me who still gets snappy when I'm tired, who sometimes doubts, who isn't always the patient mom or perfect wife. He saw all that and said, "I want her in My family, and I'll pay whatever it takes." If He loved me at my worst, why would He love me any less now that I'm His? In fact, the Bible says nothing can separate us from His love (Romans 8:38–39).

So I began to exhale. I let go of a lot of the frantic striving. I started serving from a place of calling and joy rather than fear and obligation. When you know you're secure in God's love, you serve Him out of gratitude, not to score points. And that is a game changer, friends.

Perhaps you've been living under the weight of trying to make God happy. If you are in Christ, know this week that He is already pleased to call you His. You don't have to hustle for His approval. You and God can be "good."

Reflection Questions

- Do you ever feel like you have to "perform" for God or earn His love through good behavior, service, prayer, etc.? What might God be saying to you about that mindset?

- How would your life look different if you were absolutely convinced that God delights in you and that you have nothing to prove?
- Write down two or three affirmations straight from Scripture about your identity in Christ and recite them this week. Some examples include, "I am a beloved child of God" (1 John 3:1), "I am forgiven" (Ephesians 1:7), or "I am God's masterpiece" (Ephesians 2:10).

The Least of These

*Truly I tell you, whatever you did for one of the least
of these brothers and sisters of mine, you did for me.*
—Matthew 25:40

WHEN I FIRST stepped into the child welfare world, I got hit between the eyes with the hard truth that I had been living in a comfortable bubble, largely unaware of the suffering right in my own community. As I sat in the lobby of the child welfare office, I saw things that wrecked me.

I remember a thirteen-year-old girl arriving at the office with literally nothing but the clothes on her back. She'd been removed from her home for her safety. She was scared, angry, and had no belongings. No toothbrush, no pajamas, no favorite stuffed animal to cling to. I sat with her and witnessed her fear and confusion. In that moment, something shifted in me. It was no longer possible to pretend that "those kinds of problems" were far away. They were right here, in my town, practically in my lap. And I had a choice to either look away or lean in.

Jesus has a way of turning our eyes to the margins if we're willing. In the Bible, He constantly gravitated toward the vulnerable and famously said, "Whatever you did for one of the least of these brothers and sisters of mine, you did for Me." That means when we feed someone hungry, welcome a stranger, care for the sick or imprisoned, it's as if we're doing it to Jesus Himself.

Conversely, ignoring "the least" is ignoring Jesus. Oof. That realization made me take a hard look at my circle. The reality is that if all your friends look like you, and none of them qualify as the least of these, then we have to get out of our comfort zone and go love on the least of these.

God used that teenage girl and many kids after her to tug me out of complacency. My husband and I became foster parents, and later we adopted, because we could no longer stand by knowing children were sleeping in offices or bouncing between placements. Did it complicate our lives? Oh, yes. Did it bless our lives? More than words can say.

Those experiences taught me that our faith isn't truly lived out until it costs us something and blesses someone else. And here's the surprising thing. As we've poured out, we've been filled up with joy and purpose like never before. There's nothing quite like knowing you were able to be Jesus's hands and feet for someone in need.

Now, not everyone is called to foster or adopt, but I firmly believe every one of us is called to engage with "the least of these" in some way. It might be as simple as finally learning your elderly neighbor's story and helping them with groceries. It could be volunteering at a shelter or becoming a mentor to at-risk youth. It might be stepping out of your predominantly comfortable social circle and befriending someone who's from a different background. We won't know who God wants us to love until we intentionally look around beyond our usual crowd.

Reflection Questions

- Jesus is calling us to love beyond our comfort zone. Who are "the least of these" in your community or daily life?
- What is one practical way you can step beyond your usual boundaries this season to serve or befriend someone in one of those difficult situations?
- If you already serve in a ministry to the vulnerable, what keeps you motivated? If you feel burnout or discouragement, pray and ask God to show you glimpses of His presence in those you serve.

Fall

Learn from the Wisdom of Others

The way of fools seems right to them,
but the wise listen to advice.
—PROVERBS 12:15

HAVE TO CONFESS, I felt pretty smug as we drove home from the beach after fall break. The sun was shining, the kids were laughing, and I was in full mom mode. While on fall break, my seventeen-year-old daughter rolled her eyes at my constant reminders not to forget sunscreen.

Of course, she ignored me. Day one at the beach, she skipped the SPF. By day two, my strong-willed girl was burnt to a crisp—looking like a cheap, peeling leopard-print handbag. Sometimes, even when wisdom is waving a big red flag, we think, "That won't happen to me." Well, it happened. And I couldn't resist an "I told you so" (delivered with love and maybe a tiny grin). It got me thinking: *Why can't we learn from the wisdom of others?*

Isn't that the million-dollar question? How often do we hear a story about someone's mistake or pain and still march off to learn things the hard way ourselves? In my daughter's case, she had literal proof from her mother's life experience about sunburns, but she still had to feel the sting on her own skin.

When I think about it, how many times has God lovingly warned me through Scripture or the advice of wise people, and I've basically said, "Thanks, but I'll figure it out myself"? When I do, the situation never ends well. Just like my daughter learned sunburns are real, I've learned that ignoring God's wisdom leads to unnecessary heartache.

I imagine our heavenly Father watching us with the same mix of frustration and compassion I felt as a mom. He's given us plenty of examples in His Word, all so we don't have to repeat the same mistakes. From Adam and Eve reaching for that forbidden fruit to the Israelites grumbling in the desert, the Bible is full of lessons if we're willing to listen. God must shake His head affectionately and think, "Child, if you would only trust Me on this, you could save yourself some pain."

These days, I'm praying for a more teachable spirit. What if I decided to take God at His word and also heed the godly counsel of those who have gone before me? Proverbs 12:15 says, "The way of fools seems right to them, but the wise listen to advice." I don't want to be that fool with the peeling nose (literally or figuratively). I want to be wise. That means swallowing my pride and learning from others' experiences instead of charging ahead blindly. It means when my mom or mentor shares a warning, I pause and consider that maybe God is speaking through them to protect me.

So here's to all of us learning secondhand instead of by second-degree burns. Let's choose humility over hubris. This week, when someone offers wisdom, let's listen. God places people in our lives to guide us. We'll still have to live our own lessons, but maybe we can avoid a few blisters on the way.

Reflection Questions

- Can you recall a piece of advice or biblical lesson you ignored, and what happened as a result? What might have changed if you had listened?
- In what area of your life are you insisting on learning the hard way right now? How could you seek out and heed wise counsel instead?

- Who has God placed in your life as a source of wisdom? Consider thanking them and asking God for a humble heart to learn from their experience.

Me Be Ghost, Say Boo!

*If you are willing and obedient, you will
eat the good things of the land.*
—ISAIAH 1:19

'LL NEVER FORGET when our family survived Halloween with a threenager, and let me tell you, it was a spectacle. For a month, my three-and-a-half-year-old proudly announced to anyone who'd listen: "Me be ghost, say BOO!" (translation: he wanted to be a ghost for Halloween). Now, Mom-brain here tried every which way to gently dissuade him. I offered beloved character costumes, superhero getups, you name it. No dice. "Me be ghost, say boo!" he insisted, over and over.

Fine. I finally caved and bought a ghost costume, which was basically a white sheet with eye holes. Immediately, I thought, *This is a terrible idea.* Sure enough, our first trunk-or-treat event arrived, I excitedly slipped the sheet over his head, and he FREAKED OUT!

He couldn't see well, felt smothered, and was stumbling around. He ripped it off, screamed bloody murder, and said, "No! Don' wanna be ghost! Don' wanna!" So there we were in the church parking lot with a hysterical ghost who had transformed back into a kid in regular clothes, because his costume was tied around his neck like a makeshift cape. Sigh. He ended up happily running from car to car yelling "Boo!" at people while not actually wearing the ghost outfit.

As I collapsed into bed that night, a thought hit me: *Lord, is this what we look like to You?* I mean, here was my stubborn preschooler adamant about doing something his way, despite my guidance. And when he finally got what he wanted, it was a disaster, and who had to rescue him? Mom. It reminded me of how many times I've pestered God for something or barreled ahead with my plan, only to end up uncomfortable and crying, "Lord, help!"

God lays out in His Word the best way to live—for our well-being, not His kicks. "Love your enemies." "Keep the Sabbath." "Flee from temptation." And so on. But we often respond like my son: "No, I'm gonna do it my way!" We insist on our own will, like a toddler demanding a ghost costume. And when it inevitably leaves us short of breath, tripping in the dark, we yell, "God, why'd You let this happen?!"

I picture God shaking His head with a gentle chuckle, thinking, *Child, if only you had listened.* Isaiah 1:19 says, "If you are willing and obedient, you will eat the good things of the land." In other words, if you trust and obey God's ways, you'll experience the best He has. I ended up quoting that verse to myself: "Ronda, if you obey, you'll feast on God's goodness. If you rebel, well, you'll be eating dirt under a hot ghost costume."

So there are two "moral of the story" takeaways I gleaned. First, don't sweat the small stuff with kids. Honestly, by kid number four, I'm so much more chill. Second, stop fighting God's guidance. How many times have I metaphorically insisted on a "ghost costume" God knew would bring me grief? Too many.

That night, after my son was snoring soundly (clutching the ghost costume he had refused to wear), I prayed: "Lord, enough of my tantrums. Help me to yield to Your better way up front, instead of learning the hard way." That is a prayer we all can pray this coming week.

Reflection Questions

- Can you identify an "I'll do it my way" moment in your life that ended up being a flop? What did you learn from it about God's wisdom versus your own?

- In what areas do you sense God has been gently nudging you to trust His instructions? What would it look like to say, "Okay, Lord, I'll take off my 'ghost costume' and follow Your lead"?
- If you're a parent or leader, where might you be majoring in the minors? Are there ghost-costume-level battles you can let go of in order to focus on guiding in more meaningful areas?

Sunday 41:

Thankful in the Face of Anxiety

*Do not be anxious about anything, but in
every situation, by prayer and petition, with
thanksgiving, present your requests to God.*
—Philippians 4:6

THANKSGIVING IS MY absolute favorite holiday. I love the turkey, the pie, the gathering of friends and family, and the fact that there's no pressure of buying presents. But I know not everyone feels the warm fuzzies this time of year. For many, Thanksgiving can stir up anxiety. Family tensions, high expectations, or loneliness can sneak in alongside the mashed potatoes. As we headed into the holiday recently, I found myself worrying about loved ones who struggle with anxiety. How could I help them feel peace when life feels overwhelming?

Around that time, I attended a conference where a speaker named Toby shared his journey with severe anxiety. He's a strong believer who found himself battling panic attacks in his mid-thirties. As a mom, I hung on his every word, hoping to glean how I might better support my anxious teen. Toby said something that surprised me when he noted that science has proven that practicing gratitude each day can actually lower anxiety. Basically, even one intentional moment of thankfulness can start to rewire our brains toward contentment. He shared how he began a habit of speaking out one "I am" statement

149

from Scripture daily—reminding himself of his identity in Christ—and coupling it with simple thanks to God. It struck me that God's been telling us this all along in His Word!

Philippians 4:6 says, "Do not be anxious about anything, but in every situation, by prayer and petition, with thanksgiving, present your requests to God." God invites us to bring our worries to Him through prayer, but also to intentionally season those prayers with gratitude. It's not that thanking God magically erases problems. But gratitude shifts our focus off our fears and onto His goodness. It's pretty hard to spiral in anxiety while you're busy thanking God for a warm home, a loyal friend, or simply the breath in your lungs.

So our family decided to test this out in a fun way. Every evening at dinner, we now do "happys and crappys." Each person shares one thing they're thankful for and one challenge from the day. Let me tell you, even on the hard days, hearing my kids dig up one thing that made them smile brings a noticeable peace around the table. It hasn't cured anxiety in our home, but it's creating a refuge of joy that anxiety struggles to penetrate. We're training our hearts to see God's hand in everything, big or small.

This week, no matter what circumstance you find yourself in, I challenge you to start a daily thank-you habit. Maybe each morning, before your feet hit the floor, name one thing you're grateful for. Or each night, jot down three blessings in a journal. Don't worry if they seem trivial. Watch how this simple discipline can brighten your mood and bolster your faith. Gratitude is like a little seed that grows and crowds out the weeds of worry. It reminds us that God has been and will continue to be faithful, no matter what tomorrow holds.

Reflection Questions

- What is one worry that's been weighing on you? Take a moment to pray about it, and include three specific "thank-yous" to God within that prayer.

- Start a simple gratitude ritual this week, such as a nightly thankfulness list or dinnertime sharing. Who could you invite to join you in this practice?
- Think of a past stressful situation where God provided for you or taught you something. How can remembering that circumstance and thanking Him for it help you face current anxieties with more peace?

Sunday 42:

Letting Go and Letting God

*Great peace have those who love your law,
and nothing can make them stumble.*
—Psalm 119:165

I ONCE MADE A promise to myself that if I ever saw a gorgeous sunrise at the beach, I'd raise my hands in praise like that iconic image of a man worshipping in the waves. Well, when the moment came, I froze. I was standing ankle-deep in the ocean at dawn, heart pounding, completely self-conscious.

What would people think? Was anyone watching? I almost missed my chance because I was afraid of looking silly. Finally, I took a deep breath, shut out the world, and lifted my hands high. In that vulnerable act of surrender, an incredible peace washed over me. The worries about others' opinions melted away, and it was just Jesus and me, in perfect harmony.

That morning taught me a powerful lesson. Sometimes you have to let go of fear and obey God, even if it feels uncomfortable, in order to experience His peace. My hesitation on the beach was about more than raised hands. It was about trust. Deep down, I was grappling with letting go of control. Can you relate? Maybe God's nudging you to do something that scares you, but you're stuck, worrying about "what ifs" and people's opinions. I've been there. But I'm learning that on the other side of obedient surrender is a freedom you can't find anywhere else.

153

Consider King David in the Bible. He was so uninhibited in worship that he danced with all his might before the Lord (much to his wife's embarrassment). David understood that genuine worship sometimes means looking a little foolish to the world. When I finally thrust my hands upward at the sky, I imagined heaven cheering, not because of the motion itself but because of the heart behind it. I was essentially saying, "God, You're worth my embarrassment. I yield to You." And God met me there with the gift of His presence and peace.

Psalm 119:165 says, "Great peace have those who love your law, and nothing can make them stumble." In letting go of my pride and loving God through obedience, I stumbled right into a great peace that morning. Letting go and letting God is not a one-time deal. It's a daily posture. For me, it can be as small as biting my tongue instead of snapping back in an argument, or as big as saying yes to an opportunity I feel unqualified for.

Every time I choose surrender over self-will, I feel that familiar flutter of fear as I move out of my comfort zone! But I also start to feel excitement, because I've seen that God shows up. He steadies me, guides me, and blesses my steps. Often, the situation I dreaded becomes a source of joy or growth.

This week, is God asking you to lift your hands in surrender in some area? Maybe it's literally in worship, or maybe it's a metaphor for trusting Him with your children, your career, your future. I encourage you to release that white-knuckle grip. Raise your hands and say, "Lord, I'm letting go. I'm Yours." You might be surprised at the immediate relief that floods your soul.

Reflection Questions

- What "raised hands" moment is God inviting you into? Identify one step of obedience you've been hesitant about due to fear or pride.

- Recall a time you surrendered control and later experienced God's peace or provision. How does remembering that encourage you to trust Him now?
- Are you more concerned with what others think or what God desires? Pray for the courage to prioritize God's voice over public opinion, even if it feels uncomfortable.

I See You and I'm Here

*For we do not have a high priest who is
unable to empathize with our weaknesses, but
we have one who has been tempted in every
way, just as we are—yet he did not sin.*
—Hebrews 4:15

LATELY GOD HAS been impressing on my heart the power of empathy. Not just sympathy, which might say, "Aw, I feel sorry for you," but real empathy, which actually enters into someone's pain and says, "I get it, and I'm here with you."

A while back, I watched a little animated video by researcher Brené Brown that humorously illustrates the difference. In the video, a person is stuck down in a deep, dark hole. Sympathy peers down from above and says, "Ooh, it looks scary down there. So sorry you're stuck. Need a sandwich?" Meanwhile, empathy climbs down a ladder into that hole, sits next to the person, and says, "I've been here before. You're not alone." Isn't that exactly what Jesus did for us?

The ultimate act of empathy, of course, was the Incarnation itself. The king of heaven put on human flesh and all its frailties. Jesus felt hunger, exhaustion, and physical pain. He experienced frustration, sadness, and betrayal by close friends. Why? So that no one could ever say, "God, You just don't understand what I'm going through." He does understand. Completely. When you cry out to Jesus, you're talking to Someone who has walked in your shoes.

That brings me so much comfort. It also challenges me. Because if Jesus climbed down into the hole with us, then I, as His follower, need to be willing to do the same for others.

Flashy programs or perfect words aren't what heal people, but presence does. Simply being with someone in their pain, listening, and affirming that they're not crazy for hurting, is a gift. It reflects Jesus's heart.

Often we want to solve people's problems or avoid the discomfort of their suffering. But much of the time, what hurting people need most is just not to be alone in it. A friend who sits and cries with you will often minister more than a friend who only offers cheery platitudes from a distance.

This week, practice the ministry of "I see you, I'm here." Is there someone in your life going through a hard time? Maybe a coworker overwhelmed by life, a friend battling depression, or even your child facing struggles at school? Instead of giving quick advice or expressing sympathy from afar, try drawing on your own experiences to empathize.

You may not have the exact same story, but you can probably relate to the core feelings of fear, loneliness, disappointment, or shame. Sometimes a simple, "I've been through something similar, and it was really hard. I'm here for you," can be a lifeline to someone drowning in pain. As you step out of your comfort zone to extend empathy, Jesus shows up.

In that moment, you become His hands and feet, and His love flows through you to the other person.

Reflection Questions

- Who in your life right now is hurting or struggling? Identify one person you can intentionally reach out to with empathy. How might you let them know, "I see you, and I'm here," this week?

- When have you experienced someone else's empathy during a tough time? How did their willingness to "climb down into the hole" with you make a difference in your healing or comfort?
- Are you hesitant to share your own struggles with others? What fears hold you back? Pray about one area of vulnerability that, if shared appropriately, could help someone else feel less alone.

Take Every Thought Captive

We take captive every thought to
make it obedient to Christ.
—2 CORINTHIANS 10:5B

I HAVE A BUSY mind. If my thoughts were depicted as a place, it'd be like Times Square on New Year's Eve—bustling, loud, confetti flying everywhere. Especially in stressful seasons, my brain can fill with worries, to-do lists, and the occasional self-critical voice that sounds eerily like a mix of my middle school frenemy and the enemy of my soul.

Recently, I realized I was letting those rogue thoughts run wild way too often. In a candid moment, I told a friend, "I think half my exhaustion is coming from the thoughts running through my brain." She nodded knowingly and then asked, "Have you tried fighting those thoughts with truth?" She reminded me of 2 Corinthians 10:5, about taking every thought captive for Christ. I knew the verse, but I wasn't exactly practicing it. My mind was like an open-door party where any anxious or negative thought could waltz in and make itself at home. It was time to become a more discerning bouncer at the door of my mind.

That week, I started a new habit. Whenever I caught an ugly thought coming in, I would literally say (sometimes out loud, if no one was around), "Hold up! Who sent you?" If the thought was not aligned with God's truth or character, it didn't get a free pass to linger. For example, when a thought whispered, "This situation is hopeless,"

I answered it with, "Actually, with God all things are possible. He's helped me before and He'll do it again." If a thought sneered, "You're failing," I replied, "Even if I fall short, God's grace is sufficient, and His power is made perfect in weakness. I'm loved regardless." And y'all, it made a difference.

Instead of being bullied by my thoughts, I began bossing them around in Jesus's name. It felt weird at first, even tiring (I had no idea how many negative thoughts I entertained until I started catching them!). But over time, the atmosphere of my mind started to shift. Peace inched in, worry edged out. I realized I don't have to accept every thought that pops up; I have Holy Spirit authority to reject lies and choose truth. What a relief!

If you struggle with runaway thoughts, know that you are *not* at their mercy. With God's help, you can take those thoughts captive and run them through the Philippians 4:8 filter of whatever is true, noble, right, pure, lovely, or admirable. If it passes that test, think on it. If it's from the pit, send it back to where it came from.

Your mind is a battlefield, but you don't fight alone or unarmed. God's given you His Word and His Spirit, so use them. Times Square mind or not, with God you can cultivate a mentality that honors Him this week—one captive thought at a time.

Reflection Questions

- What negative or anxious thought tends to frequent your mind? Identify one recurring thought and find a biblical truth that directly counters it.
- Consider your mental "input." Are there sources that feed your fears or insecurities? How might you set healthy boundaries there while you work on renewing your mind?
- This week, practice "thought auditing." At the end of each day, jot down any worrisome or harmful thoughts you noticed and how you responded. What changes do you notice in your peace or perspective over time?

We Need Each Other

*Two are better than one, because they have a
good return for their labor: If either of them
falls down, one can help the other up.*
—ECCLESIASTES 4:9–10

ONCE HAD THE chance to speak at a church in Knoxville about Isaiah 117 House. Before I went up, the pastor read a familiar verse from Ecclesiastes about how two are better than one. As I listened from the front pew, my mind wandered back to a night that changed my life. It was the night a nine-month-old baby boy named Isaiah was placed in our care.

I remember getting the call around 3:30 p.m. "There's an infant who needs a foster home. Can you take him?" My husband and I said yes, hopped in our minivan with our two kids, and headed to the Department of Children's Services to meet our new little guy.

Now, I am *not* a planner, and at that moment that fact was painfully obvious. I had a nine-year-old and a twelve-year-old at home. No babies. Which meant I had zero baby supplies on hand. No crib, no diapers, no formula, nothing. That reality didn't hit me until we were buckling this sweet, chubby-cheeked boy into our car.

I panicked internally. *What am I going to do?* All I knew was to call my friend Amy and ask her to pray for us. Well, Amy did a lot more than pray. Unbeknownst to me, she rallied our entire small group of church friends, and by the time we pulled into our driveway with Isaiah, cars were lining up behind us. Friends arrived almost simultaneously, arms full of baby essentials.

Amy showed up with a baby bathtub (It was pink, but who cares?), and baby wash and a cute little outfit she'd just bought. Another friend came with a high chair, someone else brought a crib and set it up, others brought diapers, wipes, formula, clothes, even cash to help with whatever we needed. In the span of an hour, our living room looked like a fully stocked nursery. I stood in the middle of that chaos of generosity and nearly cried from gratitude.

I also remember thinking a sobering thought: If Isaiah's biological mom had even a fraction of this community supporting her, he might not have needed foster care at all. That thought has stuck with me. Community can literally be life-changing.

God never meant for us to go through hard times alone. The Bible paints a picture of believers supporting one another, carrying each other's burdens, practicing hospitality, praying together. That night I experienced the church being the church in the most tangible way. My friends couldn't fix all of our new challenges, but they made sure we didn't face them by ourselves.

God created us to be relational, just as He is relational. Jesus surrounded Himself with disciples and friends. He broke bread with people and attended weddings and went fishing with the guys. He taught crowds, yes, but He also spent intimate time with a close-knit group. When I think of how irritable and impatient society feels right now, I suspect a big part of it is loneliness and lack of true community. We're not designed to carry life's stresses alone, and when we try, it warps us a little. We become quicker to snap and slower to extend grace.

This week, as you reflect on your relationships, ask God to show you one person or group you can reach out to. It could be as simple as sending a text to someone you haven't seen in a while or as bold as inviting a new family over for dinner.

And if you are the one feeling isolated, I encourage you to take a deep breath, say a prayer, and take a proactive step. Maybe call up a friend or let your church know you'd like to get connected. We were never meant to do life alone.

Reflection Questions

- In what ways have you been relying on virtual connections (social media, texting) instead of real-life community? What is one thing you could do to foster a face-to-face friendship or fellowship this week?
- Can you think of a time when friends, family, or church community supported you during a tough season? How did their presence impact you, and how might you offer that to someone else now?
- Who is one person in your life who might be feeling alone or isolated right now? What practical step can you take to reach out to them and remind them that they don't have to go through life alone?

When Challenges Become Blessings

*Fixing our eyes on Jesus, the pioneer and perfecter
of faith. For the joy set before him he endured
the cross, scorning its shame, and sat down
at the right hand of the throne of God.*
—HEBREWS 12:2

GOD HAS A way of taking our trials and using them as refining fires that bring out gold. It doesn't mean those hardships magically become easy or that we have to pretend to enjoy them. But it means none of our suffering is wasted. God is always at work behind the scenes, chiseling our character, increasing our dependence on Him, and setting the stage to bless us and others through us in surprising ways.

At our Isaiah 117 Houses, we often say our greatest challenge is also our greatest blessing. Opening that red door to children in trauma is hard. Every time, you face the unknown. *What will this child need? How broken will their heart be?* It's challenging, and it stretches every volunteer.

Yet, every time, we also experience this sacred blessing. We get to lavishly love a child who desperately needs it. In those hardest moments—comforting a toddler at 2 a.m. or cleaning up the tears of a teenager—the presence of God is so near it's almost tangible. The veil between heaven and earth feels thin, and we sense God's pleasure. Truly, the blessing of seeing a frightened child smile or relax for the first time far outweighs the exhaustion.

Maybe you're facing a challenge right now that has you thinking, "This might break me." I've thought that before. But I can testify, and so can countless others, that with God's help, your biggest challenge can become your biggest blessing. It might become the testimony that gives someone else hope. It might forge an unshakeable faith in you that couldn't come any other way. Or it might simply make you more like Jesus, who knew all about challenges and somehow, for "the joy set before him," endured even the cross for our sake.

If I could go back and tell my younger self anything, I'd say: "Don't be so afraid of hard things. Embrace them with courage, knowing God is in it with you, and something beautiful is being born." My family's foster journey was full of tears and unknowns, but I see now it was also full of God's glory—in our home, in my kids, in that little boy's life. Our hearts got broken and enlarged. Our challenge became a blessing.

So hang in there this week. Lean into God like never before amid that challenge. Ask Him to open your eyes to glimpses of the good He's bringing out of it. You might not see the full picture for a while, and that's okay. Trust that He's working. One day you may even thank Him for that trial, strange as it sounds now. Because on the other side of it, you'll realize you're walking a little closer with Him, shining a little brighter with His love, and that is a blessing that lasts.

Reflection Questions

- Reflect on a past hardship in your life. In hindsight, can you identify any ways God used that challenge to bring about growth, good, or blessing for you or others?
- What current challenge are you facing that you can surrender to God's purposes? Take a moment to tell God you trust Him to bring good from it, even if you can't see it yet.

- How can you turn this perspective outward? Is there someone going through a hard time whom you can encourage with the hope that God can transform challenges into blessings?

Sunday 47:

Don't Give Up on Church

And let us consider how we may spur one another
on toward love and good deeds, not giving up
meeting together, as some are in the habit of
doing, but encouraging one another—and all
the more as you see the Day approaching.
—Hebrews 10:24–25

SIX SUNDAYS. THAT'S how long I stayed away from church a while back. I didn't intend for it to be that long; it just sort of happened. One weekend we were traveling for a family event, the next I was speaking out of town, then one Sunday I just couldn't bring myself to go. I was weary and, if I'm honest, nursing some hurt feelings from a previous church experience.

I'll just watch a sermon online, I told myself. That turned into a month and a half of solo Sundays. Then one Sunday morning, a dear friend gently invited me to come with her to her church. I hesitated, but something nudged me to accept. So I slipped into a back row of an unfamiliar church, feeling oddly nervous and hoping no one would notice me.

To my surprise, that service melted the ice around my heart. When it came time for Communion, an usher handed me the little cup and wafer, and my eyes filled with tears. There I was, sitting among believers again, about to take the Lord's Supper. The pastor spoke about

Jesus's body broken for our sins, His blood shed to make us new, and it hit me hard: *I need this. I need Him. And I need these people to walk this journey with me.*

In that moment, God reminded me why Hebrews 10:25 urges us not to give up meeting together. Church isn't a nice-to-have social club. It's oxygen for our faith. It's God's design that we pursue Him in community, not in isolation.

Now, I know church can be *messy*. Boy, do I know. I've experienced misunderstandings, disappointments, even betrayal at the hands of fellow Christians. It hurts especially because we expect better from "church people." You might be reading this with some deep church wounds of your own. If so, hear me tenderly: I'm not downplaying that pain. People in the church can at times show a very wrong picture of Jesus. But I also want to encourage you with what God had to remind me: Don't give up on the church because some sinners, just like you and me, have done a bad job living out its mission.

The Church (with a capital *C*) is Jesus's beloved bride, warts and all. He hasn't given up on her, and He hasn't given up on *you*. As the world grows darker and more chaotic, we need each other more, not less! We need to spur one another on toward love and good deeds, to encourage one another in our struggles, to sing and pray side by side. Yes, even with off-key singers and quirky personalities and all.

If you've been distant from church, can I gently challenge you to give it another try this week? I'm not saying the first Sunday back will be magical. It might be awkward, or you might still feel a little guarded. That's okay. But keep going. Find a Bible-teaching, Jesus-loving community and you might just find that you need the Church, and the Church needs you!

Reflection Questions

- If you've been hurt or disappointed by a church or other believers, have you talked to God? What might taking a step toward healing and forgiveness look like in your situation?

- How has being part of a church community (now or in the past) helped you in your walk with God? Can you identify one positive impact that Christian fellowship has had on your life?
- Hebrews 10:25 calls us to encourage one another. Who is one person at your church you can encourage this week with a kind word, a note of appreciation, or a prayer together?

Sunday 48:
Breaking Down Walls with a Warm Meal

*Share with the Lord's people who are
in need. Practice hospitality.*
—ROMANS 12:13

AT ISAIAH 117 House, I've seen firsthand that sometimes the simplest things can open a hardened heart. I remember a teenage girl who came into one of our homes around Thanksgiving. She had been through so much trauma and showed up angry at the world. I'm talking arms crossed, walls up, one-word answers.

Our team commenced lavish love! Giving her space but letting her know we cared. On Thanksgiving Day, one of our volunteers invited this teen to help prepare the holiday meal. The girl had a special request: "Can we have ham with pineapple? My grandma always did that." So ham with pineapple it was! Together, she and location leader basted that ham, studded it with pineapple rings, and set the table just so. She even mentioned a home economics class where she learned table settings, and we said, "Go for it, make it pretty!"

As we all sat down to eat, I watched a transformation. This tough young lady, who initially wouldn't speak or meet our eyes, began to soften. Over oven mitts and pineapple slices, her guard came down. She shyly shared a few memories of her grandmother. She even managed a small smile when we complimented her table decor. It was like a little crack of light in a dark room. By the end of dinner, she was chatting with the staff and other kids, visibly more relaxed than when she arrived. All it took was a home-cooked meal and a place at the table.

That Thanksgiving, I relearned an old truth that hospitality heals. In the Bible, we see hospitality over and over. Jesus was constantly sharing meals with sinners, tax collectors, friends, even Pharisees. And those meals often led to deep heart changes. In our case, a ham with pineapple became God's tool to show a lonely teenager that she still mattered, that she could contribute and belong.

Sometimes we think serving God has to be grand or complicated. But setting an extra place at your table, offering a warm cup of coffee, and inviting someone into your ordinary routine are holy acts. They create space for God to work. In the safe atmosphere of a shared meal, burdens can ease and stories can surface. I saw it happen with that young woman. The kitchen became a classroom of grace for her and for us. Her walls didn't crumble entirely in one day, but significant cracks appeared, all because she felt at home.

So ask yourself this week: *How can I bring a hospitality mindset into my everyday life?* Maybe it's inviting the new neighbor over for pizza, even if my living room is a toy war zone. Or welcoming the awkward coworker to eat lunch with me rather than alone. Or pausing to truly listen to the elderly woman in the grocery line. Let's open our doors to others, remembering that the simplest welcome can lead to the most profound healing.

Reflection Questions

- Can you think of a time when someone's hospitality made you feel especially valued or comforted? What elements of that experience could you emulate for others?
- Who in your life or community might be feeling "on the outside" or lonely right now? What is one thing you could do to extend hospitality or inclusion to them?

- Sometimes we hesitate to open our homes or lives because things are messy or imperfect. What fear or obstacle holds you back from practicing hospitality?

Ask God How to Spend Your Time

*If any of you lacks wisdom, you should ask
God, who gives generously to all without
finding fault, and it will be given to you.*
—JAMES 1:5

THE TURKEY LEFTOVERS were barely put away when I felt that familiar holiday hustle creeping in. Christmas music blared in every store and my calendar was suddenly overflowing with school plays, work parties, and shopping lists. My heart started racing with the pressure of it all. How would I get everything done and still be merry?

Then, one chaotic afternoon, I found myself at my five-year-old's basketball game, watching a herd of kindergarteners attempt free throws. It took ages to get them lined up, and just as one little guy was about to shoot, a parent hollered, "Who's blocking out the free-throw shooter?!" Folks, these kids could barely aim the ball at the hoop. I had to laugh, and thought: *What are we doing? Why are we treating a kids' game like the NBA finals? Why am I treating the holidays like a frantic race?*

Sitting there on the bleachers, I felt God gently tap on my heart. There's a better way. Instead of letting the world's pace sweep me away, I could ask God how He wants my family and me to spend our time. Revolutionary idea, huh? We often pray about big decisions, but what about our schedules?

James 1:5 says, "If any of you lacks wisdom, you should ask God, who gives generously to all without finding fault, and it will be given to you." I certainly needed wisdom on what to say "yes" or "no" to in that season. So I did something radical. I actually prayed about my calendar. "Lord, show me what's important to You for us these next five weeks. Where do You want our energy and resources to go?" And then (this is key), I paused to listen.

Almost immediately, I sensed a shift. Ideas stirred in my mind: Instead of trying to attend every single event, maybe host a simple get-together to really connect with friends. Instead of searching for perfect presents, involve the kids in making a few heartfelt gifts. I even felt prompted to schedule a family "PJ day" with no plans except cookie baking and a Christmas movie. And guess what? I felt relief. It was as if God was saying, "Permission granted to slow down."

When we ask God how to spend our time, we're essentially acknowledging that every day is a gift from Him. I used to approach my planner like a puzzle I had to solve on my own. Now I'm learning to approach it more like a prayer list. Before filling every slot, I ask, "God, is this something You want for us? Will this bring my family closer to You or to each other? Show me what to prioritize."

If the thought of doing this makes you nervous, remember: God doesn't want to steal our fun. He wants to maximize our joy by focusing us on what's meaningful. When we follow His lead, we often find ourselves at the right place at the right time, with enough energy to be fully present. The world will always shout about what we "must do" to have a great holiday or a successful life. But only God truly knows the best use of our days. He can see the future and the ripple effects of each "yes" and "no." Who better to consult with on your schedule this week?

Reflection Questions

- Take a look at your upcoming week or month. Have you invited God into those plans? What is one practical way you can ask for His guidance?
- Identify one activity or commitment that has been draining rather than life-giving. Pray for wisdom: Is this something God is asking you to let go of to make room for something better or even for rest?
- Conversely, is there something nudging your heart that you haven't made time for—like a coffee with a friend, a day off, or serving someone in need? How might God be directing you to prioritize that?

Surrender Your Perfect Plans

"Martha, Martha," the Lord answered, "you are
worried and upset about many things, but few things
are needed. . . . Mary has chosen what is better."
—LUKE 10:41-42

I HAVE A CONFESSION. I nearly killed Christmas. Not the actual holiday, mind you, but one particular December Sunday, I orchestrated such a stressful morning that my family wondered if "peace on earth" had skipped our house entirely. Here's what happened. In my zeal to honor Jesus, I had this brilliant idea to volunteer my two little boys (ages six and eight) to sing at both church services as part of the Advent worship. Without asking anyone, I signed them up.

This will be a perfect way to celebrate Jesus, I assumed. Fast-forward to that Sunday morning and the boys were tired and cranky from a late night, my husband and I were frantically ironing tiny button-down shirts, and we had to rush out the door to get to church early. Tensions were high. In the church foyer, with fifteen minutes until go-time, my husband and I had a not-so-soft-spoken "discussion" about which one of us was responsible for this chaos.

By the time the kids went up to sing, we parents were emotionally exhausted and a little irritated with each other. To add insult to injury, one of my boys refused to open his mouth on stage, while the other scowled the whole time. So much for my brilliant idea.

Later, over an emergency post-church coffee, I had to laugh. Why did I do that? I realized I'd been a "Martha." You know Martha. The one always hustling to make everything just so, missing the point and causing Jesus to chide her in the process. In my case, I was so worried about orchestrating the "perfect" Christmas activity for Jesus that I forgot to ask Jesus if He even wanted it. The result? Stress, strife, and zero focus on the actual Savior. I suspect the Lord would've preferred I simply sat with my family in worship, rather than turning them into an unwilling children's choir.

After that fiasco, I did what I probably should've done from the start. I prayed, "Lord, what do You want our Christmas season to look like?" And wouldn't you know, the ideas that came to mind were much simpler and more joyful than my own. We felt led to have a quiet family movie night with hot cocoa one weekend, and on another, to visit a nursing home and sing carols. We also revived an old tradition of lighting an Advent candle each evening and reading a short Scripture.

Nothing Instagram-fancy, but it made our hearts slow down and remember why we celebrate. Those ended up being the holy moments, the ones where I sensed Jesus whisper, "This is the 'better' thing. Just be with Me." I needed to surrender my Pinterest-fueled picture of Christmas and embrace the messier, sweeter reality that God just wants my heart and my family's hearts, not a flawless pageant. I have even tattooed the word "surrender" on the inside of my left forearm so that every time I look down, I see the word and remember to surrender to Him!

So as you navigate busy seasons or big projects, remember my almost-ruined Christmas and take a pause. Are you doing things for God without being with God? Are you pushing a plan that He might be gently redirecting? Don't be afraid to lay it down and surrender your plans to Him.

Reflection Questions

- Can you recall a time when you, like Martha, were "worried and upset" by trying to make something perfect, and your idea backfired? What does that experience teach you about your priorities?

- What is one area in your life right now where you sense God might be asking you to surrender your plans or expectations?
- Think about the balance between serving God and sitting with God. Which do you find more challenging, and why?

Say Yes—Even When It's Scary

*Who knows but that you have come to your
royal position for such a time as this?*
—ESTHER 4:14B

AS I BRING this yearly devotional to a close, it's only fitting I go full circle and show how this devotional came about. In mid-2017, a good friend of mine kept nagging me to share updates on what God was doing in our fledging ministry. "Ronda, you need to make a video every week. Just talk about how God's moving," she insisted.

I balked. Weekly videos of myself on Facebook? Putting my face and heart out there? Umm, no thanks, I thought. But this friend wouldn't quit. Finally, I caved. In June 2017, with a mix of fear and faith, I hit the "record" button for the first *Sundays with Ronda*. I had no clue what I was doing. I figured a handful of people (mostly my mom) might watch. Little did I know I was saying "yes" to a domino effect of God-moments.

Fast-forward to today, and those weekly videos not only documented miracle after miracle in real time but also built a community. People began tuning in from all over, praying for foster kids, donating, even starting Isaiah 117 Houses in their areas—all because of some raw, chatty videos from a reluctant lady in East Tennessee. Looking back, I marvel at how close I came to saying no. I almost let fear and insecurity rob me of this adventure.

I relate a lot to Esther in the Bible. She was an ordinary girl thrust into extraordinary purpose, and at a critical moment she hesitated to speak up. Her cousin Mordecai basically said, "If you remain silent, deliverance will come from somewhere else—but who knows, maybe you are here for such a time as this?" In other words: "Say yes, Esther. God put you here for a reason." That verse gives me chills. How many times have I needed a Mordecai-like nudge to step into God's calling?

My friend was my Mordecai. She pushed me out of the cozy harbor of comfort onto the water of obedience. And I'm so grateful. It's taught me to recognize those God-nudges more readily, and here's what I've learned: If God is prompting you to do something, however small or big, He's already prepared the way.

When I finally said yes to the weekly videos, God provided the stories, the words, the audience, and the impact. It wasn't polished or perfect, but God doesn't need our perfection. He needs our participation. He can use even shaky voices and iPhone cameras to change lives.

Is there something on your heart that you've been afraid to try? Let me lovingly play the role of my pushy friend for you and say, "Do it!" If God's in it, your "yes" can unlock blessings for you and for others that you can't imagine right now.

Reflection Questions

- Can you identify a nudge from God or an opportunity He has placed before you that you've been hesitant or afraid to pursue? What's holding you back, and what would it look like to surrender that fear to God?
- Think of a time you *did* say yes to God despite feeling unprepared. What came of it? How does that past experience encourage you to trust Him for the next challenge?
- Who are the "Mordecais" or encouraging voices in your life urging you toward God's purposes? How might you respond to their encouragement?

Sunday 52:

A New Year, a Surrendered Year

In their hearts humans plan their course,
but the LORD establishes their steps.
—PROVERBS 16:9

THIS WEEK MARKS the end of our fifty-two-week journey and the start of something new. A new year is dawning, with all its blank-page promise and unknowns. I have a little New Year's ritual. I love to steal away with my journal and reflect on the past year's highs and lows, then prayerfully set intentions for the year ahead. Notice I wrote "intentions," not "resolutions." I've learned my lesson there, as I once resolved to give up coffee, and that lasted till about January 2 at 10 a.m.

As I look to the coming year, one question rises above all others, and it's something God has been pressing into my heart: "Lord, what do You want?" In other words, I'm learning to surrender my plans to His plans. If you know me, you know I'm a natural go-getter and list-maker. But experience and a few hard knocks have taught me that holding my year with open hands leads to far greater adventures with God than anything I could script.

A few years back, I sensed God challenging me not to charge into January with my neat goals but instead to pause and truly ask Him for direction. That's when He gave me the word "surrender," and that became the year I consciously let go of my comfort zone. I said yes to speaking at events way outside my small-town bubble and watched God show up mightily. I delegated more at work and saw our staff blossom in their gifts. I even surrendered some personal hurts I'd been carrying and found unexpected freedom in forgiveness. It was as if God was proving, "See what I can do when you unclench those fists, Ronda?"

Planning is good, but yielding to God is better. He sees the year in panoramic view. We see just a few feet ahead, so it makes sense to trust the One with the map! Don't get me wrong. I still use my planner (color coded, of course). But I'm trying to pencil things in and let God have the eraser.

Proverbs 16:9 is right when it says, "In their hearts humans plan their course, but the Lord establishes their steps." I picture it like a road trip. I might plan to take the highway, but God knows about the construction zone ahead and leads me on a scenic byway instead. In the moment, I might grumble, "Why are we slowing down?" But later I realize He saved me from a traffic jam or showed me a breathtaking view I'd have otherwise missed.

Just a few short years ago, I had no idea we'd be opening thirty-seven new Isaiah 117 Houses by 2025! That wasn't on my neatly laid-out agenda. But God blew our minds with opportunities and challenges we hadn't foreseen. Looking back, the richest parts of the year were often the unscripted ones where God said, "Turn here," and we obeyed. This wasn't my plan, but it was always His. And it is beautiful.

As we stand on the cusp of a new year, I invite you to join me in this simple, freeing practice. Ask God what He wants for your year, and listen. Maybe He'll speak a word or theme into your heart. Maybe He'll gently highlight something that needs to be released. Maybe He'll nudge you toward a new direction that scares you a little. Whatever it is, write it down. Pray over it. Give God your yes before you even know the details. Trust me, I have seen what God can do with a small, scared yes!

Reflection Questions:

- Take a moment to reflect on the past year. Where did you see God show up in unexpected ways that weren't part of your original plans? How does that encourage you as you surrender the new year to Him?
- What does "surrender" look like for you practically in planning your days, weeks, and year? Is there a specific plan or goal you sense God asking you to hold loosely or submit to Him for guidance?
- Spend some time in prayer asking God for a word, verse, or focus for the coming year. What do you sense He might be speaking to your heart about His desires for you? How can you keep that at the forefront as you step into the new year with faith?

Conclusion

A S WE COME to the close of this devotional journey, I want to pause and remind you that God really is in the daily. He's in the messy mornings when you spill coffee on your shirt, in the tearful nights when you wonder if you're enough, and in the quiet moments of laughter around the table.

Week by week, we've shared stories of second chances, rest, obedience, love, and hope. And in each of them, the common thread has been God's steady presence. He doesn't just show up on Sundays or in the big milestones. He delights to meet us in the ordinary moments and transform them into something sacred.

So as you step forward into whatever comes next, carry with you the truth that God has been with you in every page you've read, and He'll be with you in every future step you take. Don't let these devotionals sit idly on the shelf of memory. Let them breathe life into your routines, your relationships, and your choices.

Keep looking for His fingerprints in the small things, and keep saying yes to the nudges He gives your heart. You may be surprised at how often heaven touches earth in your everyday. My prayer is that the rhythm of finding God in the daily doesn't end here, but that it becomes the very pattern of your life.

Remember that your story is still being written. Each new week is another chance to notice God's goodness, to extend His love, and to trust His hand guiding you. When you feel weary, let these reminders pull you back to His presence. When you feel joyful, let gratitude rise and spill over to those around you. And when you feel unsure, rest in the promise that He is already in tomorrow, working for your good. Keep your eyes open, your heart soft, and your spirit expectant, because God is in the daily, and He is in you.

About the Author

RONDA PAULSON is a wife, mom, and storyteller who also serves as the founder and executive director of Isaiah 117 House. She and her college sweetheart, Corey, live in Northeast Tennessee with their four children: Sophie, Mac, Isaiah, and Eli. Two of the kids were adopted, but they like to joke they can't remember which two!

While training to become foster parents in 2014, Ronda and Corey learned that children removed from their homes often wait in offices—scared, alone, and with little to call their own. The question, "What if there were a home?" was planted in Ronda's heart. One year later, when she and Corey picked up their first foster son in those same conditions, that question became a calling. In June 2018, the first Isaiah 117 House opened its red doors in Carter County, Tennessee. Since then, the organization has expanded to over sixty locations across thirteen states, changing the way foster care begins for more than fifteen thousand children.

Known for her authenticity, humor, and passion, Ronda shares her story on stages across the country. To learn more or to connect with her about an upcoming speaking engagement, visit https://www .isaiah117house.com or email info@isaiah117house.com.

Facebook: https://www.facebook.com/isaiah117house
Instagram: https://www.instagram.com/isaiah117house
LinkedIn: https://www.linkedin.com/company/isaiah117house